BIRDS OF AMERICA

BIRDS OF AMERICA

AN ILLUSTRATED ENCYCLOPEDIA AND BIRDWATCHING GUIDE

DAVID ALDERTON

southwater

This edition is published by Southwater
Southwater is an imprint of Anness Publishing Ltd
Hermes House, 88–89 Blackfriars Road, London SE1 8HA
tel. 020 7401 2077; fax 020 7633 9499
www.southwaterbooks.com; info@anness.com
© Anness Publishing Ltd 2004

UK agent: The Manning Partnership Ltd; tel. 01225 478444;
fax 01225 478440; sales@manning-partnership.co.uk
UK distributor: Grantham Book Services Ltd; tel. 01476 541080;
fax 01476 541061; orders@gbs.tbs-ltd.co.uk

North American agent/distributor: National Book Network; tel. 301 459 3366;
fax 301 429 5746; www.nbnbooks.com

Australian agent/distributor: Pan Macmillan Australia; tel. 1300 135 113; fax 1300 135 103;
customer.service@macmillan.com.au

New Zealand agent/distributor: David Bateman Ltd; tel. (09) 415 7664; fax (09) 415 8892

Publisher: Joanna Lorenz
Editorial Director: Helen Sudell
Project Editors: Debra Mayhew and Catherine Stuart
Designer: Nigel Partridge
Illustrators: see picture acknowledgements, below
Editorial Reader: Lindsay Zamponi
Production Controller: Darren Price
Material in this book was previously published as part of a larger volume,
The World Encyclopedia of Birds & Birdwatching
1 3 5 7 9 10 8 6 4 2

Picture Acknowledgements:

Photographs appearing on front cover, clockwise from top-left: sun conure (*Aratinga
solstitialis*) and red and green macaw (*Ara chloroptera*) supplied by Dennis Avon; bald eagle
(*Haliaetus leucocephalus*) and brown pelican (*Pelecanus fuscus*) supplied by Ardea.
Back cover, from left: blue-chested hummingbird (*Polyerata amabilis*) and beryl-spangled
tanager (*Tangara nigroviridis*) supplied by Dennis Avon.

**The Publisher would like to thank
the following picture agencies for
granting permission to reproduce
their images in this book.**
Key: l = left, r = right, t = top,
m = middle, b = bottom

Ardea: 2, 6tr, 7, 10tl, 10br, 12br, 13b,
17m, 17b, 18tr, 19br, 20bl, 21tl, 21b,
22b, 23tr, 23b, 24t, 24bl, 25t, 25b,
27t, 27b, 29m, 29b, 30t, 30b, 33,
34b, 35t, 35m, 36, 37t, 37m, 38, 39,
42t, 46bl, 46br, 48tl, 48b, 50t, 50b,
52t, 54b, 56, 58t, 60b, 61tr, 66tm,
66tr
Dennis Avon: 41t, 62, 63
NHPA: 24br, 25br, 31m
Oxford Scientific Films: 6b, 9, 14t,
15tl, 15ml, 16t, 16b, 19bl, 22t, 23tl,
26t, 28t, 31tr, 31b, 35b, 37b, 41b,
42m, 42b, 44t, 46t, 48tr, 52b, 54t,
58b, 60t, 61tl, 61b, 66tl

**All artworks by Peter Barrett
except:**

Anthony Duke: 40; all maps,
pp66–125
Studio Galante: 90, 91, 106, 107,
110, 111, 122, 123
Martin Knowelden: 8, 9, 10, 11, 15,
17, 18, 19, 20, 26, 28, 32, 36, 43, 45,
47, 49, 51, 53, 55, 57, 59, 64
Janos Marffy: 66
Andrew Robinson: 78, 79

CONTENTS

INTRODUCTION

Birds have been a source of fascination and inspiration to people since the dawn of history. Birds' mastery of the skies not only inspired humans to invent flying machines but also helped facilitate the development of modern aircraft, since airplane designers borrowed the aerodynamic features of birds to revolutionize aircraft used in intercontinental travel.

Birds have also influenced our cultures in a spiritual sense, as indicated, for example, by the thunderbird legends of the native North Americans. The feathers of various parrots, especially the majestic multi-colored macaws, continue to adorn ceremonial head-dresses and other garments, as part of the traditions of various Central American tribal people. Other occurrences reflect the role of birds as harbingers of the seasons. The reappearance of migrants from southern wintering grounds, such as the scarlet tanager (*Piranga olivacea*), is eagerly anticipated every North American springtime, as a sign of the approaching warmer weather.

It may seem surprising, but there are still new species of birds being discovered every year. Among the most recent is a new bald-headed parrot from the Mato Grosso region of Brazil, reported for the first time

Below: Birds have adapted to live, feed and breed in a wide range of different habitats. Here a puffin (Fratercula arctica) *is returning from a successful fishing trip at sea.*

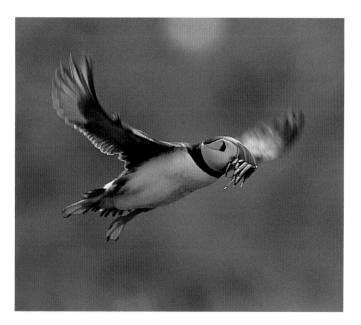

Above: Rheas are the largest birds found in America today, and are confined to the southern continent where they roam the grassland areas. They stand about as tall as an adult person.

in July 2002. As an approximate guide, there are over 9,000 avian species present on Earth—a total far in excess of the number of mammals. There is virtually no environment on the planet where birds are not to be seen, even in the freezing wasteland of Antarctica, where penguins maintain a remarkable vigil to breed in one of the most inhospitable environments to be found anywhere on Earth.

Birds have spread so widely over the planet's surface not only because of their ability to fly, but also because they are highly adaptable in their feeding habits. Birds eat a wide variety of foods, ranging from microscopic plankton to the carcasses of large mammals, as well as all types of vegetable matter and numerous invertebrates.

In recent years, human activities have had an increasingly harmful impact on numerous avian populations around the world, and are now threatening the very survival of many species. On the bright side, however, technology is being applied as never before to assist the survival of critically endangered species such as the Californian condor (*Gymnogyps californianus*), giving real hope for such birds' survival in what may hopefully become a more enlightened era of human activity.

Birdwatching has also benefited from technological advances, such as the Internet, which enables information about new sightings to be relayed instantly to

enthusiasts. Undoubtedly, webcam opportunities to observe bird sites even on the other side of the world will increase in the years ahead. Yet one of the reasons why birdwatching has become such a popular pastime is that it can be carried out basically anywhere. No special equipment is necessarily required, although binoculars, sketchpads and similar items can add greatly to your enjoyment and understanding of avian life.

This book is a celebration of birds that sets out to reveal the diversity that exists in both their form and lifestyles. The second part features species that can be observed throughout America, and off the shores of these two continents. Each bird is placed within the geographical context in which it is most likely to be seen. Even if you do not have the opportunity to visit the lush rainforests of the Amazon basin, or the Alaskan tundra, you will still be able to marvel at the diversity of American avian life, as portrayed in these pages.

Below: Secure nesting sites are important for the survival of all birds. This Harris's hawk (Parabuteo unicinctus) *has bred successfully, with its nest being protected by a thorny cactus.*

THE ORIGINS OF BIRDS

Vertebrates—first flying reptiles called pterosaurs, and later birds—took to the air about 190 million years ago. Adapting to an aerial existence marked a very significant step in vertebrate development, because of the need for a new method of locomotion, and a radically different body design.

The age of *Archaeopteryx*

Back in 1861, workers in a limestone quarry in Bavaria, southern Germany, unearthed a strange fossil that resembled a bird in appearance and was about the size of a modern crow, but also had teeth. The idea that the fossil was a bird was confirmed by the clear evidence of feathers impressed into the stone, as the presence of plumage is one of the characteristic distinguishing features of all birds. The 1860s were a time when the debate surrounding evolution was becoming fierce, and the discovery created huge interest, partly because it suggested that birds may have evolved from dinosaurs. It confirmed that birds had lived on Earth for at least 145 million years, existing even before the age of the dinosaurs came to a close in the Cretaceous period, about 65 million years ago. As the oldest-known bird, it became known as *Archaeopteryx*, meaning "ancient wings."

Pterosaurs

A study of the anatomy of *Archaeopteryx*'s wings revealed that these early birds did not just glide but were capable of using their wings for active flight. Yet they were not the first vertebrate creatures to have taken to the skies. The pterosaurs had already successfully developed approximately 190 million years ago, during the Jurassic period, and they even shared the skies with birds for a time. In fact, remains of one of the later pterosaurs, called *Rhamphorhynchus*, have been found in the same limestone deposits in southern Germany where *Archaeopteryx* was discovered. The pterosaur's wings more closely resembled those of a bat than a bird, consisting simply of a membrane supported by a bony framework, rather than feathers overlying the skin.

Some types of pterosaurs developed huge wingspans, in excess of 23ft (7m), which enabled them to glide almost effortlessly over the surface of the world's oceans, much like albatrosses do today. It appears that they fed primarily on fish and other marine life, scooping their food out of the water in flight. Changes in climate probably doomed the pterosaurs, however, since increasingly turbulent weather patterns meant that gliding became difficult, and they could no longer fly with ease.

Above: An impression of how Archaeopteryx *may have looked. It is impossible to be sure of its coloration from its fossilized remains.*

Avian giants

In the period immediately after the extinction of the dinosaurs, some groups of birds increased rapidly in physical size, and in so doing, lost the ability to fly. Since their increased size meant that they could cover large distances on foot, and as they faced no predators, because large hunting mammals had not yet evolved, these tall birds were relatively safe. In New Zealand, home of the large flightless moas, such giants thrived until the start of human settlement about a millennium ago. The exact date of the final extinction of the moas is not recorded, but the group had probably died out entirely by the middle of the nineteenth century.

Below: The largest species of moa would have dwarfed a man.

Below: All pterosaurs had a similar body shape with a narrow head, which may have been embellished with a crest of some sort. This may have been used for display purposes and also to reduce air resistance in flight. The wing structure of pterosaurs was very different from that of birds: their wings basically consisted of skin membranes, stretched out behind the forearms.

It was this large surface area that allowed them to glide with little effort, but becoming airborne in the first place required great effort. The lack of body covering over the skin also had the effect of causing greater heat loss from the body. In birds, the feathers provide insulation as well as assisting active flight.

Below: Hoatzin chicks (Opisthocomus hoazin) are unique among today's birds in possessing claws on their wing tips, which help them to climb trees. The claws are lost by the time the birds are old enough to fly.

The spread of birds

After the age of *Archaeopteryx*, it is thought that birds continued to radiate out over the globe and became increasingly specialized. Unfortunately, there is very little fossil evidence to help us understand their early history. This lack of fossils is partly due to the fact that the small carcasses of birds would have been eaten whole by scavengers, and partly because their lightweight, fragile skeletons would not have fossilized easily. In addition, most birds would not have been trapped and died under conditions that were favorable for fossilization.

By the end of the age of the dinosaurs, birds had become far more numerous. Many seabirds still possessed teeth in their jaws, reflecting their reptilian origins. These probably assisted them in catching fish and other aquatic creatures. It was at this stage that the ancestors of contemporary bird groups such as waterfowl and gulls started to emerge. Most of the forerunners of today's birds had evolved by the Oligocene epoch, some 38 million years ago.

Some groups of birds that existed in these times have since disappeared, notably the phororhacids, which ranged widely over South America and even into parts of the southern United States. These birds were fearsome predators, capable of growing to nearly 10ft (3m) in height. They were equipped with deadly beaks and talons, and probably hunted together in groups.

Recent finds

During the mid-1990s, the discovery of avian fossils in China that were apparently contemporary with those of *Archaeopteryx* aroused considerable interest. Like its German relative, *Confuciusornis* possessed claws on the tips of its wings, which probably helped these early birds to move around. Similar claws are seen today in hoatzin chicks. *Confuciusornis* resembled modern birds more closely than *Archaeopteryx* in one significant respect: it lacked teeth in its jaws. Further study of the recent fossil finds from this part of the world is required however, as some may not be genuine.

THE SKELETON AND PARTS OF A BIRD

The bird's skeleton has evolved to be light yet robust, both characteristics that help with flight. To this end, certain bones, particularly in the skull, have become fused, while others are absent, along with the teeth. The result is that birds' bodies are lightweight compared to those of other vertebrates.

In order to be able to fly, a bird needs a lightweight body so that it can become airborne with minimal difficulty. It is not just teeth that are missing from the bird's skull, but the associated heavy jaw muscles as well. These have been replaced by a light, horn-covered bill that is adapted in shape to the bird's feeding habits. Some of the limb bones, such as the humerus in the shoulder, are hollow, which also cuts down on weight. At the rear of the body, the bones in the vertebral column have become fused, which gives greater stability as well as support for the tail feathers.

The avian skeleton

In birds, the greatest degree of specialization is evident in the legs. Their location is critical to enable a bird to maintain its balance. The legs are found close to the midline, set slightly back near the bird's center of gravity. The legs are powerful, helping to provide lift at take-off and absorb the impact of landing. Strong legs also allow most birds to hop over the ground with relative ease.

There are some differences in the skeleton between different groups of birds. The atlas and axis bones at the start of the vertebral column are fused in the case of hornbills, for example, but in no other family.

Feet and toes

Birds' feet vary in length, and are noticeably extended in waders, which helps them to distribute their weight more evenly. The four toes may be arranged either in a typical 3:1 perching grip, with three toes gripping the front of the perch and one behind, or in a 2:2 configuration, known as zygodactyl, which gives a surer grip. The zygodactyl grip is seen in relatively few groups of birds, notably parrots and toucans. African touracos have flexible toes so they can swap back and forth between these two options.

The zygodactyl arrangement of their toes helps some parrots to use their feet like hands for holding food. Birds generally have claws at the ends of their toes, which have developed into sharp talons in the case of birds of prey, helping them to catch their quarry even in flight. Many birds also use their claws for preening, and they can provide balance for birds that run or climb.

Right: The typical skeleton of a bird. Note the prominent breastbone for the attachment of flight muscles. The large area occupied by the orbit of the eye reflects the fact that birds in general rely heavily on their sense of sight.

Parrot

Above: Parrots use their feet to hold food, in a similar way to human hands.

Bird of prey

Above: In birds of prey, the claws have become talons for grasping prey.

Wader

Above: Long toes make it easier for waders to walk over muddy ground or water plants.

Duck

Above: The webbed feet of ducks provide propulsion in water.

1 Metacarpals
2 Alula
3 Ulna
4 Radius
5 Cervical vertebrae
6 Ear
7 Cranium
8 Eye socket
9 Nostril
10 Bill (upper mandible)
11 Bill (lower mandible)
12 Clavicle (wishbone)
13 Ribs
14 Sternum (breastbone)
15 Metatarsals
16 Tarsus
17 Tibia and Fibula
18 Femur
19 Humerus

Above: The narrow bill of waders such as this whimbrel (Numenius phaeopus) *enables these birds to probe for food in sand or mud.*

Above: Birds of prey such as the golden eagle (Aquila chrysaetos) *rely on a sharp bill with a hooked tip to tear their prey apart.*

Darwin's finches

In the 1830s, a voyage to the remote Galapagos Islands, off the northwest coast of South America, helped the British naturalist Charles Darwin to formulate his theory of evolution. The finches present on the Galapagos Islands today are all believed to be descended from a single ancestor, but they have evolved in a number of different ways. The changes are most obvious in their bill shapes. For example, some species have stout, crushing beaks for cracking seeds, while others have long, slender beaks to probe for insects. These adaptations have arisen to take full advantage of the range of edible items available on the islands, where food is generally scarce. Some species have even developed the ability to use cactus spines and similar items as tools to extract seeds and invertebrates. In total, there are now 12 recognized species found on these islands, and nowhere else in the world.

Above: Cranes have strong, pointed bills, which they use like daggers to seize prey such as frogs between the upper and lower parts.

Above: Flamingos have bills that enable them to feed with their heads trailing backwards in the water.

Below: The finches of the Galapagos Islands helped to inspire Charles Darwin's theory of evolution. They are thought to be descended from a common ancestor, and have diverged significantly to avoid competing with each other for food. This is reflected by their bill shapes. The woodpecker finch (Camarhynchus palidus) *has even acquired the ability to use a tool, in this case a cactus spine, to winkle out grubs hiding in tree bark.*

Above: The hyacinthine macaw (Anodorhynchus hyacinthinus) *has one of the most powerful bills of any bird.*

Above: The curved, twisted bill of the red crossbill (Loxia curvirostra) *allows these birds to extract seeds easily from pine cones.*

Bills

The bills of birds vary quite widely in shape and size, and reflect their feeding habits. The design of the bill also has an impact on the force that it can generate. The bills of many larger parrots are especially strong, allowing them to crack hard nut shells. In addition, they can move their upper and lower bill independently, which produces a wider gape and, in turn, allows more pressure to be exerted.

Wings

A bird's wing is built around just three digits, which correspond to human fingers. In comparison, bats have five digits supporting their fleshy

membranes. The three digits of birds provide a robust structure. The power of the wings is further enhanced by the fusion of the wrist bones and the carpals to create the single bone known as the carpometacarpus, which runs along the rear of the wing.

At the front of the chest, the clavicles are joined together to form what in chickens is called the wishbone. The large, keel-shaped breastbone, or sternum, runs along the underside of the body. It is bound by the ribs to the backbone, which provides stability, especially during flight. The major flight muscles are located in the lower body and provide propulsive thrust when airborne.

FEATHERS

The presence of feathers is one of the main distinguishing characteristics that set birds apart from other groups of creatures on the planet. The number of feathers on a bird's body varies considerably—a swan may have as many as 25,000 feathers, for instance, while a tiny hummingbird has just 1,000 in all.

Aside from the bill, legs and feet, the entire body of the bird is covered in feathers. The plumage does not grow randomly over the bird's body, but develops along lines of so-called feather tracts, or pterylae. These are separated by bald areas known as apteria. The apteria are not conspicuous under normal circumstances, because the contour feathers overlap to cover the entire surface of the body. Plumage may also sometimes extend down over the legs and feet as well, in the case of birds from cold climates, providing extra insulation here.

Feathers are made of a tough protein called keratin, which is also found in our hair and nails. Birds have three main types of feathers: the body, or contour, feathers; the strong, elongated flight feathers on the wings; and the warm, wispy down feathers next to the bird's skin.

A diet deficient in sulphur-containing amino acids, which are the basic building blocks of protein, will result in poor feathering, creating "nutritional barring" across the flight and tail feathers. Abnormal plumage coloration can also have nutritional causes in some cases. These changes are usually reversible if more favorable environmental conditions precede the next molt.

The functions of feathers

Plumage has a number of functions, not just relating to flight. It provides a barrier that retains warm air close to the bird's body and helps to maintain body temperature, which is higher in birds than mammals—typically between 106 and 110°F (41 and 43.5°C). The down feathering that lies close to the skin, and the overlying contour plumage, are vital for maintaining body warmth. Most birds have a small volume relative to their surface area, which can leave them vulnerable to hypothermia.

A special oil produced by the preen gland, located at the base of the tail, waterproofs the plumage. This oil, which is spread over the feathers as the bird preens itself, prevents water penetrating the feathers, which would make the bird so waterlogged that it

Below: Feathering is not only necessary for flight and insulation, it is also used for display purposes. This orange cock of the rock (Rupicola rupicola) *relies on its colorful appearance to attract a mate at a communal display ground, or "lek."*

Above: A bird's flight feathers are longer and more rigid than the contour feathers that cover the body, or the fluffy down feathers that lie next to the skin. The longest, or primary, flight feathers, which generate the most thrust, are located along the outer rear edges of the wings. The tail feathers are often similar in shape to the flight feathers, with the longest being found in the center. Splaying the tail feathers increases drag and so slows the bird down.

1 Primaries
2 Secondaries
3 Axillaries
4 Rump
5 Lateral tail feathers
6 Central tail feathers
7 Breast
8 Cere
9 Auricular region (ear)
10 Nape
11 Back
12 Greater under-wing coverts
13 Lesser under-wing coverts

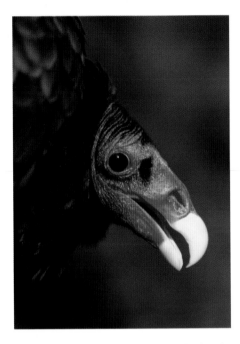

Above: The absence of feathers on the head means that carnivorous birds, such as the turkey vulture (Cathartes aura), *can feed on offal inside large carcasses without staining its plumage with blood.*

could no longer fly. The contour feathers that cover the body are also important for camouflage. Barring, in particular, breaks up the outline of the bird's body, helping to conceal it in its natural habitat.

The plumage has become modified in some cases, reflecting the individual lifestyle of the species concerned. Woodpeckers, for example, have tail feathers that are short and rather sharp at their tips, providing additional support for gripping onto the sides of trees. Vultures, on the other hand, have bare heads because plumage here would soon become stained and matted with blood when these birds fed on a carcass.

Social significance of plumage

Plumage can also be important in social interactions between birds. Many species have differences in their feathering that separate males from females, and often juveniles can also be distinguished by their plumage. Cock birds are usually more brightly colored, which helps them to attract their mates, but this does not apply in every case. The difference between the sexes in terms of their plumage can be quite marked. Cock birds of a number

of species have feathers forming crests, and others have magnificent tail plumes, such as the booted racquet-tail hummingbird (*Ocreatus underwoodii*), whose display is one of the most remarkable sights in the avian world.

Recent studies have confirmed that birds that appear relatively dull to our eyes, such as the cowbird (*Molothrus*), with its blackish plumage, are seen literally in a different light by other birds. They can visually perceive the ultraviolet component of light, usually invisible to us, making these seemingly dull birds appear greener. Ultraviolet coloration may also be significant in helping birds to choose their mates.

Molting

Birds' feathering is maintained by preening, but it becomes frayed and worn over time. It is therefore replaced by new plumage during the process of molting, when the old feathers are shed. Molting is most often an annual event. However, many young birds shed their nest feathers before they are a year old.

Molting may also be triggered by the onset of the breeding season in some species, as is the case with many finches. Cock finches usually have significantly duller plumage for much of the year, which undergoes a dramatic transformation when they are ready to breed. After losing their original feathers, they develop a new, more colorful and attractive plumage. Hormonal alterations in the body are important in triggering this process, with external factors, such as increased daylight hours, playing a part in prompting breeding behavior.

Iridescence

Some birds are not brightly colored, but their plumage literally sparkles in the light, thanks to its structure, which creates an iridescent effect. One of the particular features of iridescence is that the color of plumage alters, depending on the angle at which it is viewed, often appearing quite dark, almost black, from a side view. This phenomenon is particularly common in some groups of birds, notably members of the starling family (Sturnidae), and hummingbirds (Trochilidae), which are sometimes described as having metallic feathers because of the shimmering effect they create.

In some cases, the iridescent feathering is localized, while in others, it is widespread over most of the body. Green and blue iridescence is common, with reddish sheens being seen less often. Iridescence is especially common in cock birds, helping them to attract mates. In some cases, therefore, it is seen only in the breeding plumage, notably on the upperparts of the body and the wings rather than the underparts.

Below: A blue-chinned sapphire hummingbird (Chlorestes notatus) *displays its iridescent plumage.*

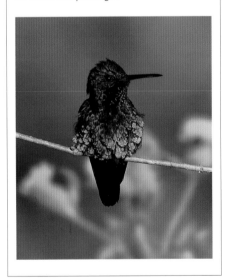

Right: The feather shaft holds the feather in place in the skin. Barbs run off the shaft at regular intervals, rather like the branches of a tree, and divide into smaller branches called barbules. Tiny hooks are attached to these, that reinforce the structure of each flight feather, making them more rigid.

Barb Barbule

Shaft

FLIGHT

*Some birds spend much of their lives in the air, whereas others will only fly as a last resort if threatened.
A few species are too heavy to take off at all. The mechanics of flight are similar in all birds, but flight
patterns vary significantly, which can help to identify the various groups in the air.*

In most cases, the whole structure of the bird's body has evolved to facilitate flight. It is important for a bird's body weight to be relatively light, because this lessens the muscular effort required to keep it airborne. The powerful flight muscles, which provide the necessary lift, can account for up to a third of the bird's total body weight. They are attached to the breastbone, or sternum, in the midline of the body, and run along the sides of the body from the clavicle along the breastbone to the top of the legs.

Weight and flight

There is an upper weight limit of just over 40lb (18kg), above which birds would not be able to take off successfully. Some larger birds, notably pelicans and swans, need a run-up in order to gain sufficient momentum to lift off, particularly from water. Smaller birds can dart straight off a perch. Close to the critical weight limit for flight, the male Kori bustard (*Ardeotis kori*) from Asia is the world's heaviest flying bird, although it prefers to run rather than fly because of the effort involved in becoming airborne.

*Below: A typical take-off, as shown by a
Harris's hawk* (Parabuteo unicinctus). *The feet
play almost as vital a role as the wings.*

Above: Birds such as the Andean condor
(Vultur gryphus) *can remain airborne with
minimum expenditure of energy, by gliding
rather than flying.*

Wing shape and beat

The shape of the wing is important for a bird's flying ability. Birds that remain airborne for much of their lives, such as albatrosses, have relatively long wings that allow them to glide with little effort. The wandering albatross (*Diomedea exulans*) has the largest wingspan of any bird, measuring about 11ft (3.4m) from one wing tip to the other. Large, heavy birds such as Andean condors (*Vultur gryphus*) may have difficulty in flying early in the day, before the land has warmed up. This is because at this stage, there is insufficient heat coming up from the

ground to create the thermal air currents that help to keep them airborne. In common with other large birds of prey, Andean condors seek out these rising columns of air, which provide uplift, and then circle around in them.

The number of wing beats varies dramatically between different species. Hummingbirds, for example, beat their wings more frequently than any other bird as they hover in front of flowers to harvest their nectar. Their wings move so fast—sometimes at over 200 beats per minute—that they appear as a blur to our eyes. At the other extreme, heavy birds such as swans fly with slow, deliberate wing beats.

Lightening the load

It is not just the lightness of the bird's skeleton that helps it to fly. There have been evolutionary changes in the body organs too, most noticeably in the urinary system. Unlike mammals, birds do not have a bladder that fills with urine. Instead, their urine is greatly concentrated, in the form of uric acid, and passes out of the body with their faeces, appearing as a creamy-white, semi-solid component.

*1. When resting, a bird
typically has a relatively
upright stance.*

*2. As it leans forwards for
take-off, it raises its wings
and starts to lift its legs.*

*3. Leaving its perch, the bird
pushes off into the air, and
opens its wings.*

Above: Hummingbirds such as this broadtail (Selasphorus platycercus) *have unparalleled aerial maneuverability, thanks to their rapid wing movements.*

Below: The black-browed albatross (Diomedea melanophris) *and its relatives often skim just above the waves.*

The aerofoil principle

Once in flight, the shape of the wing is crucial in keeping the bird airborne. Viewed in cross-section from the side, a bird's wing resembles an airplane's wing, called an aerofoil, and, in fact, airplanes use the same technique as birds to fly.

The wing is curved across the top, so the movement of air is faster over this part of the wing compared with the lower surface. This produces reduced air pressure on top of the wing, which provides lift and makes it easier for the bird to stay in the air.

The long flight feathers at the rear edge of the wings help to provide the thrust and lift for flight. The tail feathers, too, can help the bird remain airborne. The kestrel (*Falco tinnunculus*), for example, having spotted prey on the ground, spreads its tail feathers to help it remain aloft while it hovers to target its prey.

A bird's wings move in a regular figure-eight movement while it is in flight. During the downstroke, the flight feathers join together to push powerfully against the air. The primary flight feathers bend backward, which propels the bird forward. As the wing moves upward, the longer primary flight feathers move apart, which reduces air resistance. The secondary feathers farther along the wing provide some slight propulsion. After that, the cycle simply repeats itself.

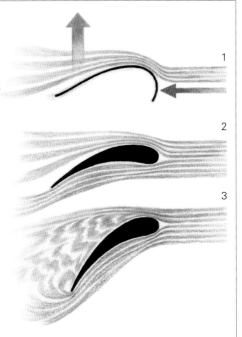

Above: The flow of air over a bird's wing varies according to the wing's position.
1. When the wing is stretched out horizontally, an area of low pressure is created above the wing, causing lift.
2. As the wing is tilted downward, the flow of the air is disrupted, causing turbulence and loss of lift.
3. When the wing is angled downward, lift slows, which results in stalling. The bird's speed slows as a consequence.

Flight patterns and formations

Different species of birds have various ways of flying, which can actually aid the birdwatcher in helping to identify them. For example, small birds such as tits (Paridae) and finches (Fringillidae) alternately flap their wings and fold them at their sides, adopting a streamlined shape, which helps to save energy. This produces a characteristic dipping flight. Large birds such as ducks and geese maintain a straighter course at an even height.

In some cases, it is not just the individual flying skills of a bird that can help it to stay airborne, but those of its fellows nearby. Birds flying in formation create a slipstream, which makes flying less effort for all the birds behind the leader. This is why birds often fly in formation, especially when covering large distances on migration.

4. Powerful upward and downward sweeps of the wings propel the bird forwards.

5. When coming in to land, a bird lowers its legs and slows its wing movements.

6. Braking is achieved by a vertical landing posture, with the tail feathers spread.

LOCOMOTION

For most birds, flight is the main means of locomotion. However, the ability to move on the ground or in water can be vital, particularly when it comes to obtaining food. Some birds have even lost the ability to fly, relying instead on their swimming or running skills to escape predators and find food.

Not all birds possess the ability to fly, but this does not mean they are handicapped in their natural environment. Penguins may appear to be rather clumsy shuffling around on land, but they are extremely well adapted to life in the water. Like other primarily aquatic birds, their webbed feet enable them to swim very effectively. Webbing is a common feature seen in aquatic birds. The skin folds linking the toes turn the foot into an effective paddle, allowing the bird to maximize its propulsive forward thrust by pushing against the water. On land, however, webbed feet do impose certain restrictions, because being linked together in this way means that the individual toes are not as flexible.

Aquatic locomotion
When penguins dive, their sleek, torpedo-shaped bodies allow them to swim fast underwater, reaching speeds equivalent to 25mph (40km/h). Their flippers, which evolved from wings,

Below: A group of king penguins (Aptenodytes patagonicus) *leap in and out of the water as they swim along, in a form of movement known as porpoising.*

help them to steer very effectively as they pursue fish, which form the basis of their diet. Like flying birds, penguins need effective wing muscles to control their movements, so their skeletal structure bears a close similarity to that of flying birds.

Flightless ducks and other aquatic birds, such as the Galapagos Island cormorant (*Nannopterum harrisi*), use a different method of locomotion: they rely entirely on their feet rather than their wings for propulsive power. Their skeletons differ from those of flying birds in that they lack the prominent keel on the sternum for the attachment of flight muscles.

Flightless land birds
A number of land birds have lost the ability to fly. Typically, they are birds that inhabit islands where, until the arrival of cats and rats brought by ships from Europe, they faced few if any predators. The arrival of predators has left them vulnerable, and many have since become extinct, including the dodo (*Raphus cucullatus*), a large, flightless pigeon from the island of Mauritius in the Indian Ocean. A high percentage of flightless birds evolved

Above: Penguins such as the chinstrap (Pygoscelis antarctica) *are less agile on land than they are in the sea, where their body shape lessens water resistance.*

on the islands of New Zealand, but many have since vanished, including all species of moa (*Dinornis* and related forms). Moas represent the most diverse group of flightless birds ever recorded. The last examples probably died out at the time of European settlement of these islands in the nineteenth century.

The giant moa (*Dinornis maximus*) was the largest member of the group and, indeed, the tallest bird ever to have existed. It would have dwarfed today's ostriches, standing up to 11$\frac{1}{2}$ft (3.5m) high. There may have been as many as a dozen or more different types of moa, which filled the same sort of niche as grazing mammals, which were absent from New Zealand.

In the absence of predatory mammals, the moas faced no significant threats to their survival until the first human settlers reached New Zealand and started to hunt them. Their large size made them conspicuous, and, having evolved in an environment where they had been safe from persecution, they had lost their ability to fly. Moas were not even able to run fast, in contrast to modern flightless birds such as ostriches. These defenseless giants were soon driven to extinction.

Circulation

The circulatory system is vital in supporting the activities of both flighted and flightless birds, ensuring that their muscles are well supplied with oxygen. The heart acts as the pump, driving the blood around the body. The basic design of the heart is similar to that of a mammal, with the left side being highly developed because it does more work. Overall, the heart rate of birds is much more rapid than mammals of similar size, having been measured at 1,000 beats per minute in the case of canaries at rest. The heart beat rises dramatically during flight, but soon returns to normal when the bird touches down.

The respiratory system

Birds have lungs, located close to the vertebral column, but these do not expand and contract in the same way as those of mammals. Instead, birds rely on a series of air sacs that act rather like bellows, to suck

air through their respiratory system. In some cases, these link with the hollow limb bones, and thus help to meet the bird's high requirement for oxygen when flying. A bird's respiratory rate is a reflection of its body size, as well as its level of activity and lifestyle. Common starlings (*Sturnus vulgaris*), for example, typically breathe about 85 times every minute, whereas domestic chickens, which are more sedentary, have an equivalent respiratory rate of only about 20 breaths per minute.

1 Trachea
2 Interclavicular air sac
3 Lungs
4 Abdominal air sac
5 Femur (leg bone)
6 Cervical air sac
7 Humerus (wing bone)
8 Anterior thoracic air sac
9 Posterior thoracic air sac

Above: The roadrunner (Geococcyx californianus) *is a fleet-footed member of the cuckoo family. It has adapted to hunting on the ground, but can fly if necessary.*

Ratites

Not all flightless birds are helpless in the face of danger, however. The large, flightless birds known as ratites, including cassowaries, ostriches, emus and rheas, are particularly well able to defend themselves. Their strong legs are quite capable of inflicting lethal blows, especially in the case of the cassowaries (Casuariidae), found in parts of northern Australia, New Guinea and neighboring islands. These birds have an elongated and deadly sharp claw on their innermost toe. If the cassowary is cornered and unable to run away, it lashes out with its legs and is quite capable of disembowelling a person with its sharp claws. The bird

also has an elongated, hard, bony crest called a casque, which protects the top of its head.

The large ratites all share a similar shape, having bulky bodies, long legs and long, slender necks. Like all flightless birds, they do possess wings, which assist them in keeping their balance and may also be used for display purposes. Most birds have four toes on each foot, but ratites have no more than three toes, and less in some cases. Ostriches have just two toes on each foot. The fastest birds on land, they can run at speeds equivalent to 31mph (50km/h). The reduction in the number of toes may help these birds to run faster.

Emus (*Dromaius novaehollandiae*) have the most rudimentary wings of all ratites, which are not even used for display purposes. The rheas (Rheidae) of South America have the most prominent wings of the ratites. They cover the rump, but they do not enable these birds to fly, even when they are young. Rheas can run if necessary immediately after hatching.

Kiwis (Apterygidae) are also ratites, but they are much smaller birds with shorter legs. Unlike other ratites, they are not fast runners, but rely on camouflage and their nocturnal habits to conceal their presence from predators, rather than speed to escape.

Running in flighted birds

Some birds that are able to fly still prefer to use their running abilities to obtain food and escape danger. They include the roadrunners (*Geococcyx californianus*) of North America. With their short wings, these birds can fly clumsily, but prefer to use their strong legs to overtake and pounce on prey. In general, flying uses considerable energy compared to running or hopping. Many birds will elect to move swiftly over the ground in order to pounce on a food item or avoid an enemy if they judge that the situation does not warrant flight.

Below: The height and keen eyesight of rheas (Rheidae) *means that they are hard to ambush in open country. Their pace allows them to escape an enemy, while their long stride length enables them to cover large amounts of ground in a single step.*

AVIAN SENSES

The keen senses of birds are vital to their survival, in particular helping them to find food, escape from enemies and find mates in the breeding season. Sight is the primary sense for most birds, but some species rely heavily on other senses to thrive in particular habitats.

Birds' senses have evolved as a result of their environment, and the shape of their bodies can help to reflect which senses are most significant to them.

Sight and lifestyle

Most birds rely on their sense of sight to avoid danger, hunt for food and locate familiar surroundings. The importance of this sense is reflected by the size of their eyes, with those of

Field of vision

The positioning of a bird's eyes on its head affects its field of vision. The eyes of owls are positioned to face forward, producing an overlapping image of the area in front known as binocular vision. This allows the owl to pinpoint its prey exactly, so that it can strike. In contrast, the eyes of birds that are likely to be preyed upon, such as woodcocks, are positioned on the sides of the head. This eye position gives a greatly reduced area of binocular vision, but it does give these birds practically all-round vision, enabling them to spot danger from all sides.

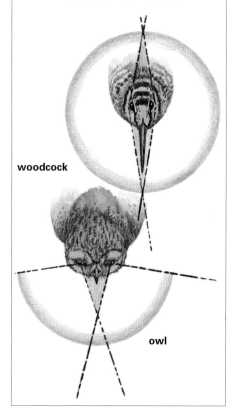

woodcock

owl

starlings (*Sturnus vulgaris*), for example, making up 15 per cent of the total head weight. The enlargement of the eyeballs and associated structures, notably the eye sockets in the skull, has altered the shape of the brain. In addition, the optic lobes in the brain, which are concerned with vision, are also enlarged, whereas the olfactory counterparts, responsible for smell, are poorly developed.

The structure of the eye also reveals much about a bird's habits. Birds of prey have large eyes in proportion to their head, and have correspondingly keen eyesight. Species that regularly hunt for prey underwater, such as penguins, can see well in the water. They have a muscle in each eye that reduces the diameter of the lens and increases its thickness on entering water, so that their eyes can adjust easily to seeing underwater. In addition, certain diving birds such as little auks (*Alle alle*) use a lens that forms part of the nictitating membrane, or third eyelid, which is normally hidden from sight. Underwater, when this membrane covers the eye, its convex shape serves as a lens, helping the bird to see in these surroundings.

Eye position

The positioning of the eyes on the head gives important clues to a bird's lifestyle. Most birds' eyes are set on the sides of the head. Owls, however, have flattened faces and forward-facing eyes that are critical to their hunting abilities. These features allow owls to target their prey.

There are disadvantages, though—owls' eyes do not give a rounded view of the world, so they must turn their heads to see around them. It is not just the positioning of owls' eyes that is unusual. They are also able to hunt effectively in almost complete darkness. This is made possible in two

Above: Vultures such as the Andean condor (Vultur gryphus) *rely on their keen eyesight and sense of smell to pick up powerful odors arising from carcasses on the ground.*

ways. First, their pupils are large, which maximizes the amount of light passing through to the retina behind the lens, where the image is formed. Second, the cells here consist mainly of rods rather than cones. While cones give good color vision, rods function to create images when background illumination is low.

The positioning of the eyes of game birds such as woodcocks (*Scolopax rusticola*) allows them to spot danger from almost any angle. It is even possible for them to see a predator sneaking up from behind. Their only blind spot is just behind the head.

Smell

Very few birds have a sense of smell, but kiwis (Apterygidae) and vultures (forming part of the order Falciformes) are notable exceptions. Birds' nostrils are normally located above the bill, opening directly into the skull, but kiwis' nostrils are positioned right at the end of the long bill. They probably help these New Zealand birds to locate

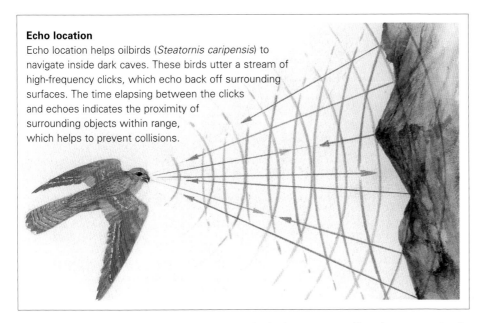

Echo location

Echo location helps oilbirds (*Steatornis caripensis*) to navigate inside dark caves. These birds utter a stream of high-frequency clicks, which echo back off surrounding surfaces. The time elapsing between the clicks and echoes indicates the proximity of surrounding objects within range, which helps to prevent collisions.

earthworms in the soil. Vultures have very keen eyesight, which helps them to spot dead animals on the ground from the air, but they also have a strong sense of smell, which helps when homing in on a distant carcass.

Taste

The senses of smell and taste are linked, and most birds also have correspondingly few taste buds in their mouths. The number of taste buds varies, with significant differences between groups of birds. Pigeons may have as few as 50 taste buds in their mouths, parrots as many as 400.

Birds' taste buds are located all around the mouth, rather than just on the tongue, as in mammals. The close

Below: Birds have good color vision. It is this sense that encourages hummingbirds, such as this long-billed starthroat (Heliomaster longirostris), to home in on red flowers.

links between smell and taste can lead vultures, which feed only on fresh carcasses, to reject decomposing meat. They may start to eat it, but then spit it out once it is in their mouths, probably because of a combination of bad odor and taste.

Hearing

Birds generally do not have a highly developed sense of hearing. They lack any external ear flaps that would help to pinpoint sources of sound. The openings to their hearing system are located on the sides of the head, back from the eyes.

Hearing is of particular significance for nocturnal species, such as owls, which find their food in darkness. These birds are highly attuned to the calls made by rodents. The broad shape of their skull has the additional advantage of spacing the ear openings more widely, which helps them to localize the source of the sounds with greater accuracy.

Hearing is also important to birds during the breeding season. Birds show particular sensitivity to sounds falling within the vocal range of their chicks, which helps them to locate their offspring easily in the critical early days after fledging.

The oilbird (*Steatornis caripensis*), which inhabits parts of northern South America, uses echo location to find its way around in the dark, rather like bats do. Unlike the sounds bats make,

however, the clicking sounds of the oilbird's calls—up to 20 a second in darkness—are clearly audible to humans. The bird interprets the echoes of its call to avoid colliding with objects in its path, although it also uses its eyesight when flying. Cave swiftlets (*Aerodramus*) from Asia, which also inhabit a dark environment, use echo location in a similar way to fly.

Touch

The sense of touch is more developed in some birds than others. Those such as snipe (*Gallinago*), which have long bills for seeking food, have sensitive nerve endings called corpuscles in their bills that pick up tiny vibrations caused by their prey. Vibrations that could suggest approaching danger can also register via other corpuscles located particularly in the legs, so that the bird has a sensory awareness even when it is resting on a branch.

Wind-borne sensing

Tubenoses such as albatrosses and petrels (Procellariiformes) have a valve in each nostril that fills with air as the bird flies. These are affected by both the bird's speed and the wind strength. The valves almost certainly act as a type of wind gauge, allowing these birds to detect changes in wind strength and patterns. This information helps to keep them airborne, as they skim over the waves with minimal effort.

Below: A combination of senses, especially touch, helps American oystercatchers (Haematopus palliatus) to detect their prey, which is normally hidden from view.

PLANT-EATERS

All over the world, many birds depend on plant matter as part of their diet, with seeds and nuts in particular providing nourishment. A close relationship between plants and birds exists in many cases. Birds fertilize flowers when feeding on nectar, and help to spread their seeds when eating fruit.

Many different types of birds are primarily plant-eaters, whether feeding on flowers, fruit, nuts and seeds, or other plant matter. Plant-eating species have to eat a large volume of food compared to meat-eating species, because of the low nutritional value of plants compared with that of prey such as invertebrates.

In the last century or so, many species have benefited from the spread of agriculture, which now provides them with large acreages of suitable crop plants to eat. These birds' feeding habits bring them into conflict with farmers when they breed rapidly in response to a swift expansion in their food supply. For example, populations of *Brotogeris* parakeets have grown significantly in certain parts of Central and South America, thanks largely to the spread of arable agriculture,

*Below: Birds such as the cactus wren (*Campylorhynchus brunneicapillus*) have a close association with particular plants. This wren not only feeds on the plants after which it is named, but also takes advantage of their protective thorns when nesting.*

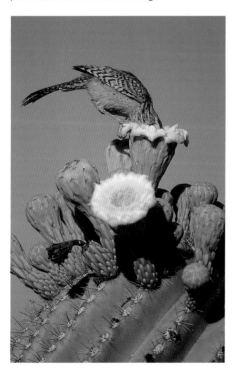

especially fruit-growing, in these regions. As feeding opportunities have increased, these small members of the parrot family have bred rapidly, and flocks are capable of wreaking havoc on crops. The birds are now considered to be pests in some areas.

Adapting to changing seasons

Birds from temperate areas exist on a varied diet that is related to the seasons. In the far north, where a blanket of snow conceals food on the ground during the winter months, willow ptarmigans (*Lagopus lagopus*) survive by feeding on buds and even the bark of dwarf willow bushes that grow in the region. During the brief northern summer, when the ground is again uncovered, they feed on flowers and other vegetation.

Some birds store plant food when it is plentiful, to sustain them through the winter. Nutcrackers (*Nucifraga*) collect hazel nuts, which they feed on in winter until the following year. Acorn woodpeckers (*Melanerpes formicivorus*) drill holes in trees that they fill with acorns, creating an easily accessible larder for the winter.

Flowers

A number of birds rely on flowers rather than the whole plant as a source of food. Pollen is a valuable source of protein, while nectar provides sugars. Not surprisingly, flower-feeders tend to be confined to mainly tropical areas, where flowers are in bloom throughout the year. Hummingbirds (Trochilidae), for instance, use their narrow bills to probe into flowers to obtain nectar. Some hummingbirds have developed especially curved or elongated bills, which allow them to feed on particular flowers. These birds help to pollinate the plants on which they feed by transferring pollen from flower to flower on their bills or even on plumage.

The digestive system

Birds lack teeth, so their food must be swallowed whole. Birds have a storage organ known as the crop, which is located at the base of the neck. From here, food passes down into the proventriculus, where the digestive process starts, before entering the gizzard, which is equivalent to the mammalian stomach. Nutrients are then absorbed through the wall of the small intestine.

The digestive system of plant-eaters differs in various respects from that of predatory species. Vegetable matter is less nourishing than meat, so plant-eaters generally need longer digestive tracts to process the large quantities of food they must consume in order to obtain enough nourishment. In addition, digesting plant matter poses certain difficulties. The gizzards of seed-eating species such as many finches (Fringillidae) have especially thick muscular walls, which serve to grind up the seeds.

1 Esophagus	6 Large intestine
2 Crop	7 Liver
3 Proventriculus	8 Spleen
4 Pancreas	9 Small intestine
5 Gizzard	

Above: Feeding on plants comes at a price, as many contain potentially harmful chemicals. Various parrots, such as these macaws (Ara species), make daily visits to cliffs to eat clay, which is believed to have a detoxifying effect on their digestive systems.

Honeycreepers, who belong to the tanager family (Thraupidae) of Central America, fill a similar evolutionary role to hummingbirds, with whom they share their small size and bright color. Unlike hummingbirds, however, they are unable to feed in flight, but have to perch within reach of the flower, sometimes pecking at the base to obtain nectar. Flowers are also a dietary favorite of some American members of the parrot family, such as the small *Touit* parrotlets, who may choose to eat them whole.

Fruit

Exclusively frugivorous (fruit-eating) birds such as fruit doves (*Ptilinopus*) are found only in the tropics, where fruit is available throughout the year. These species usually dwell in tropical rainforests, where they have a valuable role to play in protecting the biodiversity of the forest. The seeds of the fruits they eat pass right through their digestive tracts, unharmed, to be deposited far from the parent plant, which helps the plants to spread.

Plant matter

Relatively few birds feed almost entirely on herbage, although the bizarre hoatzin (*Opisthocomus hoazin*) from the rainforest of South America is one example. Its gut can become so distended with leaves that it has difficulty flying. Vegetation tends to feature quite prominently in the diets of many waterfowl too—the floating plant duckweed (*Lemna*) is so-called because of its attraction to these birds.

The breakdown of vegetation presents considerable difficulty, since birds do not possess the necessary enzymes to digest the cellulose in plants. Birds such as grouse (Tetraoninae), which feed regularly on plant matter, have evolved long, blind-ending tubes known as caeca. These contain beneficial microbes that can break down cellulose.

Nuts and seeds

These dry foods are a valuable resource to many different types of birds. However, cracking the tough outer shell or husk can present a problem. Finches such as grosbeaks have evolved a particularly strong bill, and often succeed in cracking the pit (stone) of a fruit to extract the edible kernel within. The hyacinthine macaw (*Anodorhynchus hyacinthinus*) has a bill strong enough to crack Brazil nuts.

Above: Willow ptarmigans (Lagopus lagopus) have to be versatile in their feeding habits, because of the marked climatic change that takes place in their habitat between summer and winter. Their white plumage disguises their presence when snow is on the ground.

The most bizarre example of bill adaption for eating seeds is seen in the crossbills (*Loxia*) of northern coniferous forests. These birds have literally twisted upper and lower mandibles, which help them to crack open the seeds inside the larch cones, which they eat. Some cockatoos such as the Moluccan (*Cacatua moluccensis*) have bills that are even strong enough to open coconuts.

Below: Canadian geese (Branta canadensis) can be a problem in agricultural areas, since they will sometimes descend in large numbers to graze on young cereal crops.

PREDATORS AND SCAVENGERS

Just as with other vertebrates, there is a food chain within the avian kingdom. Some species hunt only other birds, while others seek a more varied range of prey, including, commonly, invertebrates. Even birds that feed mainly on seeds catch protein-rich insects to feed their chicks in the nest.

Some avian predators feed mainly on other birds, as typified by the merlin or pigeon hawk (*Falco columbarius*) which preys on small coastline waders. Many predatory birds hunt when food is plentiful but scavenge when their prey becomes scarce. Both hunters and scavengers have evolved to live in a wide range of environments, and display correspondingly diverse hunting skills to obtain their food.

Birds of prey have sharp bills that enable them to tear the flesh of their prey into strips small enough to swallow. Eating whole animals can potentially cause digestive problems for these birds because of the bones, skin, feathers and other relatively indigestible body parts. Owls overcome this problem by regurgitating pellets composed of the indigestible remains of their prey. Kingfishers produce similar pellets of fish bones and scales. These are of value to zoologists studying the feeding habits of such birds.

Below: Peregrine falcons (Falco peregrinus) *are adept aerial hunters, with pigeons—including homing pigeons—featuring prominently in their diet. These birds of prey display not just speed, but also superb maneuverability in flight, when pursuing their quarry.*

Birds of prey

Some avian predators feed mainly on other birds, such as the sparrowhawk (*Accipiter nisus*)—which is so-called because of its preference for hunting house sparrows (*Passer domesticus*). Another avian hunter, the peregrine falcon (*Falco peregrinus*), is among the most agile of all hunting birds. Strength is a feature of some species that prey on mammals, such as the golden eagle (*Aquila chrysaetos*), which can lift young lambs in its powerful talons, but often feeds on carrion. Yet other birds of prey target different groups of vertebrates,

Above: Vision is the main sense that allows most birds of prey, such as golden eagles (Aquila chrysaetos), *to target their victims. These eagles have keen sight.*

including fish and reptiles, while a great many species hunt insects and other invertebrates.

Hunting techniques

Many predatory birds hunt during the day, but not all, with most owls preferring to seek their prey at night. Mice and other creatures that are caught by owls are killed and eaten immediately. In contrast, Old World shrikes (Laniidae) have a grisly reputation because they kill more prey than they can eat immediately. They store the surplus as a so-called larder. They impale invertebrates such as grasshoppers, and even sometimes small vertebrates, onto sharp vegetation, and return to feed on them later. Caching, as this behavior is known, is especially common during the breeding period, and presumably developed as a way of ensuring that the shrikes have sufficient food to rear their young.

Some birds have evolved particular ways of overcoming prey in certain localities. In parts of Egypt, for example, eagles have learned to prey

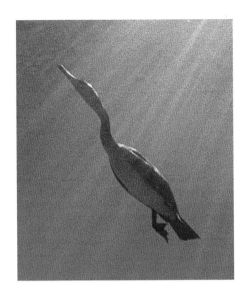

Above: Like other cormorants, the white-necked cormorant (Phalacrocorax carbo) *brings fish that it catches underwater up to the surface before swallowing them.*

Cormorants (Phalacrocoracidae) dive down after fish, and can remain submerged for some time. Kingfishers (Alcedinidae) have sharp eyesight. Having detected the presence of a fish from the air, they dive into the water, seizing their quarry in their pointed bill and then re-emerging immediately. They then kill the fish by battering it against their perch. The speed at which the kingfisher dives provides the necessary momentum to break through the surface, and it closes its wings once submerged to reduce resistance.

Aquatic predators always try to swallow their prey, such as fish, head-first. That way, gills and scales do not get stuck in their throat. On land, predatory birds that hunt victims such as rodents employ a similar technique so they do not choke on fur and tails.

Scavengers

Vultures are the best-known of all scavengers. They can home in on carcasses from a great distance away, and so have become regarded as harbingers of death. Lammergeiers (*Gypaetus barbatus*), have developed a technique that allows them to feed on bones that their relatives cannot break open. They smash the bones into pieces by dropping them from a great height. It is a skill that they learn to perfect by choosing the right terrain on which to drop the bones.

The small Egyptian vulture (*Neophron percnopterus*) survives by using its small size, which is no match

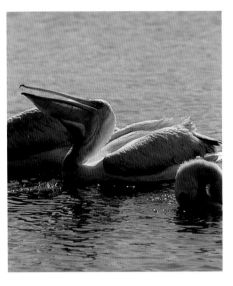

Above: American white pelicans (Pelecanus erythrorhynchos) *have expandable pouches that allow them to trawl for fish, and other edible items, in a variety of aquatic habitats.*

at the site of a kill, to advantage: it can become airborne soon after dawn—before the thermal air currents needed by its larger relatives have been created—and seek out overnight casualities. In some parts of Africa, these vultures smash tough ostrich eggs by repeatedly throwing stones at them.

Birds other than vultures also scavenge on occasion rather than hunting. Road kills of birds and other animals offer rich pickings for a host of such species, ranging from corvids such as crows and magpies to road-runners (*Geococcyx californianus*).

Below: Griffon vultures (Gyps fulvus) *and similar scavengers are able to spot a carcass on the ground using their keen eyesight, possibly combined with a sense of smell.*

on tortoises by seizing the unfortunate reptiles in their talons, and then dropping them onto rocky ground from the air to split open their shells.

Not all birds of prey are aerial predators. Species such as secretary birds (*Sagittarius serpentarius*), which range widely across Africa in grassland areas, prefer to seek their victims on the ground. Secretary birds have developed long, strong legs and yet have surprisingly small feet. Snakes feature prominently in the diet of these birds, which raise their wings when confronting one of the reptiles. This has the effect of breaking up the bird's outline, making it harder for the snake to strike. Meanwhile the bird uses its feet to stun the reptile by jumping up and down on it, before killing it with a stab of its sharp bill.

Aquatic predators

The osprey (*Pandion haliaetus*) is an unusual bird of prey that literally scoops up large fish swimming close to the water's surface while in flight. Other birds actually enter the water in search of their prey. They may not have sharp talons, but many have powerful bills that enable them to grab slippery fish without difficulty.

Pelicans are equipped with a large, capacious pouch beneath the lower part of their bill, which they use like a net to trawl the water for fish.

DISPLAY AND PAIRING

Birds' breeding habits vary greatly. Some birds pair up only fleetingly, while others do so for the whole breeding season, and some species pair for life. For many young cock birds, the priority is to gain a territory as the first step in attracting a partner. Birds use both plumage and their songs to attract a mate.

A number of factors trigger the onset of the breeding period. In temperate areas, as the days start to lengthen in spring, the increase in daylight is detected by the pineal gland in the bird's brain, which starts a complex series of hormonal changes in the body. Most birds form a bond with a single partner during the breeding season, which is often preceded by an elaborate display by the cock bird.

Bird song

Many cock birds announce their presence by their song, which both attracts would-be mates and establishes a claim to a territory. Once pairing has occurred, the male may cease singing, but in some cases he starts to perform a duet with the hen, with each bird singing in turn.

Singing obviously serves to keep members of the pair in touch with each other. In species such as Central and

Above: A male ruff (Philomachus pugnax) *at a lek, where males compete with each other in displays to attract female partners. Ruffs do not form lasting pair bonds, so the hens nest on their own after mating has occurred.*

Below: An American bittern (Botaurus lentiginosus), *well disguised in a reed bed. In spite of being solitary by nature, these waders have a remarkable territorial call, which booms out across the marshes, and has led to species becoming known locally as "Thunder-pumpers." The boom is created by use of the gullet to amplify sound, rather like a voice box.*

Below: A cock ruffed grouse (Bonasa umbellus) *displaying. The male is using his wings to create a loud drumming sound, uttering a series of quieter calls at the same time, in a bid to attract females. Drumming occurs at dawn and dusk, usually with pauses of about five minutes between displays.*

South American wood quails (*Odontophorus*), the pair coordinate their songs so precisely that although the cock bird may sing the first few notes, and then the hen, it sounds as if the song is being sung by just one bird. Other birds may sing in unison. In African gonoleks (*Laniarius*), it may even be possible to tell the length of time that the pair have been together by the degree of harmony in their particular songs.

Studies have revealed that young male birds start warbling quite quietly, and then sing more loudly as they mature. Finally, when their song pattern becomes fixed, it remains constant throughout the bird's life.

It is obviously possible to identify different species by differences in their song patterns. However, there are sometimes marked variations between the songs of individuals of the same species that live in different places. Local dialects have been identified in various parts of a species' distribution, as in the case of gray parrots (*Psittacus erithacus*) from different parts of Africa. In addition, as far as some songbirds are concerned, recent studies

Above: Black-necked swans (Cygnus melanocoryphus) *of South America normally mate for life. Pairs typically breed on their own, but once the nesting period is over, large numbers unite to form great flocks of as many as 200 individuals—a spectacular sight on large stretches of water.*

have shown that over the course of several generations, the pattern of song can alter markedly.

Birds produce their sounds—even those species capable of mimicking human speech—without the benefit of a larynx and vocal cords like humans. The song is created in a voice organ called the syrinx, which is located in the bird's throat, at the bottom of the windpipe, or trachea.

The structure of the syrinx is very variable, being at its most highly developed in the case of songbirds, which possess as many as nine pairs of separate muscles to control the vocal output. As in the human larynx, it is the movement of air through the syrinx that enables the membranes here to vibrate, creating sound. An organ called the interclavicular air sac also plays an important role in sound production, and birds cannot sing without it. The distance over which bird calls can travel is remarkable— up to 3 miles (5km) in the case of some species, such as bellbirds (*Procnias*) and the American bittern (*Botaurus lentiginosus*), which has a particularly deep, penetrating song.

Breeding behavior

Many birds rely on their breeding finery to attract their mates. Some groups assemble in communal display areas known as leks, where hens witness the males' displays and select a mate. A number of species, ranging from cocks of the rock (*Rupicola*) to birds of paradise (Paradisaeidae), establish leks.

In other species, such as the satin bowerbird (*Ptilonorhynchus violaceus*), the male constructs elaborate bowers of grass, twigs and similar vegetation, which he then decorates with items of a particular color, such as blue, varying from flowers to pieces of glass. Male bowerbirds are often polygamous,

meaning that they mate with more than one female. African weaver birds, such as the orange bishop (*Euplectes orix*), demonstrate the same behavior. The males molt to display brightly colored plumage at the onset of the breeding season, and construct nests that are inspected by the females. Hens are often drawn to the older cocks, whose nest-building abilities are likely to be more sophisticated.

Pair bonding

Many male and female birds form no lasting relationship, although the pair bond may be strong during the nesting period. It is usually only in potentially long-lived species, such as the larger parrots and macaws, or waterfowl such as swans, that a life-long pair bond is formed.

Pair bonding in long-lived species has certain advantages. The young of such birds are slow to mature, and are often unlikely to nest for five years or more. By remaining for a time in a family group, therefore, adults can improve the long-term survival prospects of their offspring.

Below: Two greater male sage grouse (Centrocercus urophasianus) *circle each other at a lek. These prominent displays help watching hens to choose a partner. There are usually just one or two dominant males with whom the hens mate: younger males—also present—are likely to be ignored. Lekking takes place from early dawn to late morning.*

NESTING AND EGG-LAYING

All birds reproduce by laying eggs, which are covered with a hard, calcareous shell. The number of eggs laid at a time—known as the clutch size—varies significantly between species, as does egg coloration. Nesting habits also vary, with some birds constructing very elaborate nests.

The coloration and markings of a bird's eggs are directly linked to the nesting site. Birds that usually breed in hollow trees produce white eggs, because these are normally hidden from predators and so do not need to be camouflaged. The pale coloration may also help the adult birds to locate the eggs as they return to the nest, thus lessening the chances of damaging them. Birds that build open, cup-shaped nests tend to lay colored and often mottled eggs that are camouflaged and so less obvious to potential nest thieves.

Nesting holes

Many birds use tree holes for nesting. Woodpeckers (Picidae) are particularly well equipped to create nesting chambers, using their powerful bills to enlarge holes in dead trees. The diameter of the entry hole thus created

Above: A northern flicker (Colaptes auratus)—*a member of the woodpecker family—returns to its nest hole. Tree holes offer relatively safe nesting retreats, although predators such as snakes may sometimes be able to reach them.*

Below: African ostriches lay the largest eggs in the world, which can weigh up to 3.3lb (1.5kg). In comparison, a chicken's egg, shown in front of the ostrich egg, looks tiny. The egg nearest to the viewer is a hummingbird egg. These tiny birds lay the smallest eggs in the avian world, weighing only about 0.01oz (0.35g).

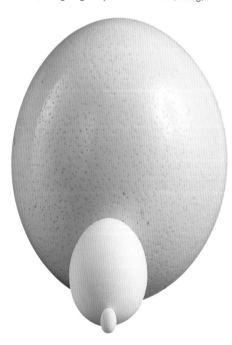

is just wide enough to allow the birds to enter easily, which helps to prevent the nest being robbed. Old World hornbills (Bucorvidae) go one stage further—the cock bird walls the hen up inside the nest. He plasters the hole over with mud, leaving just a small gap through which he can feed the female. The barrier helps to protect the nest from attacks by snakes and lizards. The female remains entombed inside until her young are well grown. At this stage she breaks out and then helps her mate to rear the chicks, having walled them back up again.

Nest-building

Some birds return to the same nest site each year, but many birds simply abandon their old nest and build another. This may seem a waste of effort, but it actually helps to protect the birds from parasites such as blood-sucking mites, which can otherwise multiply in the confines of the nest. Most birds construct their nests from vegetation, depending on which

The reproductive systems

The cock bird has two testes located within his body. Spermatozoa pass down the vas deferens, into the cloaca and then out of the body. Insemination occurs when the vent areas of the male and female bird are in direct contact during mating. Cock birds do not have a penis for penetration, although certain groups, such as waterfowl, may have a primitive organ that is used to assist in the transference of semen in a similar way.

Normally only the left ovary and oviduct of the hen bird are functional. Eggs pass down through the reproductive tract from the ovary. Spermatozoa swim up the hen's reproductive tract, and fertilize the ova at an early stage in the process. Generally, only one mating is required to fertilize a clutch of eggs. Spermatozoa may sometimes remain viable in the hen's body for up to three weeks following mating.

1 Kidneys
2 Testes
3 Vas deferens
4 Cloaca

5 Ova
6 Infundibulum

7 Magnum
8 Isthmus
9 Egg with shell contained in the hen's reproductive tract
10 Cloaca

Male **Female**

materials are locally available. In coastal areas, some seabirds use pieces of seaweed to build theirs. Artificial materials such as plastic wrappers or polystyrene may be used by some birds.

Nest styles

Different types of birds build nests of various shapes and sizes, which are characteristic of their species. Groups such as finches build nests in the form of an open cup, often concealed in vegetation. Most pigeons and doves construct a loose platform of twigs. Swallows are among the birds that use mud to construct their nests. They scoop muddy water up from the surface of a pond or puddle, mold it into shape on a suitable wall, and then allow it to dry and harden like cement.

The simplest nests are composed of little more than a pad of material, resting in the fork of a tree or on a building. The effort entailed in nest construction may reflect how often the birds are likely to nest. The platforms of pigeons and doves can disintegrate quite easily, resulting in the loss of eggs or chicks. However, if disaster does befall the nest, the pair will often breed again within a few weeks. At the other end of the scale, albatrosses expend considerable effort on nesting, because if failure occurs, the pair may not breed again for two years or so.

Cup-shaped nests are more elaborate than platform nests, being usually made by weaving grasses and twigs together. The inside is often lined with soft feathers. The raised sides of the cup nest lessen the likelihood of losing eggs and chicks, and also offer greater security to the adults during incubation. The hollow in the nest's center is created by the birds compressing the material here before egg-laying begins.

Suspended nests enclosed by a domed roof offer even greater security. They are less accessible to predators because of their design and also their position, often hanging from slender branches. Some African waxbills (*Estrilda*) build a particularly elaborate nest, comprising two chambers. There is an obvious upper opening, which is

Above: The piping plover (Charadrius melodus) *from North America breeds in the open and so must also rely on camouflage to hide its presence when sitting on the nest.*

always empty, suggesting to would-be predators that the nest is unoccupied. The birds occupy the chamber beneath, which has a separate opening.

Nest protection

Some birds rely on the safety of numbers to deter would-be predators, building vast communal nests that are occupied by successive generations and added to regularly. Monk parakeets (*Myiopsitta monarchus*) from South America breed in this way. Their nests may weigh over 4cwt (200kg) or more.

Other birds have evolved more sophisticated methods not only of protecting their nests, but also of minimizing the time that they spend

incubating their eggs. Various parrots, such as the red-faced lovebird (*Agapornis pullaria*) from Africa, lay their eggs in termite mounds. The insects tolerate this intrusion, while the heat of the mound keeps the eggs warm. Mallee fowl (*Leipoa ocellata*) from Australia create a natural incubator for their eggs by burying them in a mound where the natural warmth and heat from decaying vegetation means that the chicks eventually hatch on their own and dig themselves out.

Other birds, such as the cowbirds (*Molothrus*) of North America, simply lay and abandon their eggs in the nests of other species. The foster parents-to-be do not seem able to detect the difference between their own eggs and that of the intruder, so they do not reject the cowbird egg. They incubate it along with their own brood, and feed the foster chick when it hatches out.

Birds that nest on the ground, such as the long-billed curlew (*Numenius americanus*), are especially vulnerable to predators and rely heavily on their fairly drab plumage as camouflage. Skylarks (*Alauda arvensis*) have another means of protecting their nest site—they hold one wing down and pretend to be injured to draw a predator away.

Below: Most eggs have a generally rounded shape, but seabirds such as guillemots (Uria aalge), *breeding on exposed rocky outcrops by the ocean, lay eggs that are more pointed. This shape helps to prevent the eggs from rolling over the cliff.*

HATCHING AND REARING CHICKS

Birds are vulnerable to predators when breeding, especially when they have young in the nest. The chicks must be fed frequently, necessitating regular trips to and from the nest, which makes it conspicuous. The calls of the young birds represent a further danger, so the breeding period is often short.

Most birds incubate their eggs to keep them sufficiently warm for the chicks to develop inside. Larger eggs are less prone to chilling during incubation than small eggs, because of their bigger volume. In the early stages of the incubation period, when the nest may be left uncovered while the adult birds are foraging for food, eggs can withstand a lower temperature. Temperature differences also account for the fact that, at similar altitudes, incubation periods tend to be slightly longer in temperate areas than in tropical regions.

The eggshell may appear to be a solid barrier but in fact contains many pores, which are vital to the chick's well-being. These tiny holes allow water vapor and carbon dioxide to escape from the egg, and oxygen to enter it to reach the embryo.

Incubation

The incubation period often does not start until more than one egg has been laid, and sometimes not until the entire clutch has been completed. The interval between the laying of one egg and the next varies—finches lay every

Below: A fertile chicken's egg, showing the development of the embryo through to hatching. 1. The fertilized egg cell divides to form a ball of cells that gradually develops into an embryo. 2. The embryo develops, nourished by the yolk sac. 3. The air space at the rounded end of the egg enlarges as water evaporates. 4. The chick is almost fully developed and ready to hatch. 5. The chick cuts its way out, and its feathers dry off.

day, whereas gannets may lay only one egg every six days. If incubation does not start until egg-laying has finished, the chicks will all be of a similar size when they hatch, which increases their overall chances of survival.

The cock and hen may share incubation duties, as in the case of most pigeons and doves, or just one member of the pair may incubate. This is usually the hen, but there are exceptions. With ostriches (*Struthio*

Above: Breeding in one of the coldest places on Earth means that emperor penguins (Aptenodytes forsteri) can lay only a single egg, which they incubate on top of their feet, where special blood vessels help to warm it. After hatching, the chick is carried here too.

camelus) and most other large flightless birds, it is the male who incubates the eggs and cares for the resulting chicks. Anis (*Crotophaga*) breed communally, and all members of the group share the task of incubation.

1

2

3

4

5

Nest parasites

Nest parasitism occurs on a worldwide scale, including among the various cowbirds (Molothrus) of North America. The males do not establish territories, but mate with the females at random, who then lay a single egg in the nest of a wide range of host species. The rapid development of the cowbird's egg is vital to the chick's survival: it hatches first and monopolizes food supply, leaving the natural offspring of the host species to face starvation in the nest. The success of the cowbirds' nesting strategy is such that it has led to an apparent decline in the populations of the various host species who share its habitat.

Below: A brownheaded cowbird chick (Molothrus ater) hatches before the eggs of a western wood pewee (Conotopus sordidulus). The foster parents will continue to feed the cowbird, even when the impostor dwarfs them in size.

Hatching

Incubation periods vary among species, ranging from as few as 11 days in the case of some sparrows (*Spizella*), to over 80 days in some albatrosses (Diomedeidae). Before hatching, the chick uses the egg tooth on the tip of its upper bill to cut through the inner membrane into the air space at the blunt end of the shell, which forms as water evaporates from the egg. The chick starts to breathe atmospheric air for the first time. About 48 hours later, it breaks through the shell to emerge from the egg.

Chicks hatch out at various stages of development, and are accordingly able to leave the nest sooner or later.

Species that remain in the nest for some time after hatching, including parrots (Psittacidae) and finches (Fringillidae), hatch in a blind and helpless state and are entirely dependent on their parents at first. Birds in this group are known as nidicolous. If not closely brooded, they are likely to become fatally chilled. In contrast, species that leave the nest soon after hatching, known as nidifugous, emerge from the egg and are able to move around on their own at this stage. They can also see, and feed themselves, almost immediately. The offspring of many game birds such as pheasants, as well as waterfowl and waders, are nidifugous, which gives them a better chance of survival, as they can run to escape from predators. Young waterfowl cannot take safely to the water at first, however, because they lack the oil from the preen gland above the base of the tail to water-proof their feathers.

Rearing and fledging

Many adult birds offer food to their offspring, even some nidifugous species. This can be a particularly demanding period, especially for small birds that have relatively large broods. Blue-gray gnatcatchers (*Polioptila caerulea*), for example, must supply their offspring with huge quantities of insects, returning with food, and to clean the nest, several times each hour.

Young birds usually leave the nest from about 12 to 30 days after hatching. However, some species develop much more slowly. Albatross chicks are particularly slow developers, spending up to eight and a half months in the nest.

When they first leave the nest, many young birds are unable to fly, simply because their flight feathers are not fully functional. If these feathers are not fully unfurled from the protective sheaths in which they emerged, they cannot function effectively. The strength of the wing muscles also needs to be built up, so it is not uncommon for young birds to rest on the sides of the nest, flapping their wings occasionally, before finally taking to the air for the first time. Chicks that

Above: The tufted titmouse (Baeolophus bicolor) is typical of many birds that leave the nest before they are able to fly effectively. The young remain hidden in vegetation and are fed by their parents in these critical early days after leaving the nest.

are unable to fly immediately on fledging remain reliant on the adults, especially the cock, for food until they become fully independent.

For some young seabirds, fledging is a particularly hazardous process. From their cliff-ledge nests, they may simply flop down on to the water, where they are at risk from drowning until they master swimming skills. If they get swept out to sea, they may be caught by predators such as killer whales.

Below: The broad and often colorful gape of chicks allows parent birds such as this northern mockingbird (Mimus polyglottos) to feed their offspring quickly and efficiently. Weak chicks that are unable to raise their heads and gape at the approach of a parent will quickly die from starvation.

SURVIVAL

The numbers of a particular species of bird can vary significantly over time, affected by factors such as the availability of food, climate, disease and hunting. When the reproductive rate of a species falls below its annual mortality rate, it is in decline, but this does not mean it will inevitably become extinct.

For many birds, life is short and hazardous. Quite apart from the risk of predation, birds can face a whole range of other dangers, from starvation and disease through to human interference or persecution. The reproductive rate is higher and age of maturity is lower in species that have particularly hazardous lifestyles, such as black-capped chickadees (*Poecile atricapilla*), who often breed twice or more a year in quick succession.

Rising and falling numbers

Some birds have a reproductive cycle that allows them to increase their numbers rapidly under favorable conditions. The Galapagos Island penguin (*Spheniscus mendiculus*) is such a species. Fluctuating sea temperatures in the Pacific—part of the El Niño phenomenon—can drive sardines, its principal food source, away from the Galapagos. Very few chicks are reared during the lean years, as the native population faces starvation. During intervening periods,

*Below: A flock of American blackbirds (*Agelaius phoeniceus*). These New World birds have adapted very well to changes in their landscape brought about by agriculture. Although regarded as pests in some areas, they do consume large numbers of harmful invertebrates.*

however, the penguin population recovers, as its food source returns. Ultimately, numbers are likely to fall, threatening the species with extinction.

Regular fall-offs in populations can occur on a cyclical basis, as shown by the case of snowy owls (*Nyctea scandiaca*) in North America. As the numbers of lemmings—the main component of the owls' diet—rise, so too does the snowy owl population. This is the result of more chicks per nest being reared successfully, rather than dying of starvation. When the numbers of lemmings fall again, due to a shortage of their food, owls are forced to spread out over a much wider area

Above: Many birds watch over their offspring when they hatch, but are ill-equipped to defend them from predators, as in the case of this male Carolina wood duck (Aix sponsa).

than normal in search of food, and their breeding success plummets accordingly. Later they gradually increase again over successive years, as the lemming population recovers.

Group living

Birds that live in flocks find mates more easily than other birds, and group life also offers several other advantages, including the safety of numbers. An aerial predator such as a hawk will find it harder to recognize and target individuals in a flying mass of birds, although stragglers are still likely to be picked off.

Coloration can also increase the safety of birds in flocks. In Florida, USA, it was not unusual to see feral budgerigar flocks made up of multi-colored individuals. The different colors reflected the diversity of color varieties that were developed through domestication. Today, however, green is by far the predominant color in such flocks, as it is in genuine wild flocks, simply because predators found it much easier to pick off individuals of other colors. Greater numbers of the

Cryptic coloration

Camouflage, also known as cryptic coloration, enables a bird to hide in its natural surroundings. It offers distinct survival benefits in concealing the bird from would-be predators. Cryptic coloration has the effect of breaking up the bird's outline, allowing it to blend in with the background in its habitat. Posture and, in particular, keeping still can also help, as movement often attracts the attention of would-be predators.

Below: The common or long-tailed potoo (Nyctibius griseus) is a nocturnal species ranging from Mexico down to Argentina. It relies upon its camouflage to conceal its presence when resting during the day.

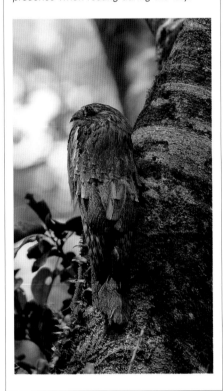

always the case. The expansion of agriculture in countries such as Argentina has resulted in the greater availability of both food and water for birds. This in turn has enabled populations, especially parrots like the Patagonian conure (*Cyanoliseus patagonus*), to grow by alarming degrees in recent years. Shooting and poisoning have been used as methods of population control, but it should be remembered that, overall, these birds have increased in numbers directly as a consequence of changes to the land pioneered by humans.

Other birds have benefited more directly from human intervention, as is the case with the common starling (*Sturnus vulgaris*). These birds have spread across North America, following their introduction from Europe in the late 1800s.

Similarly, the common pheasant (*Phasianus colchicus*) is now found across much of central North America, thanks to human interest in these game birds, which are bred in large numbers for sport shooting. Many more survive than would otherwise be the case, thanks to the attention of gamekeepers who not only provide food, but also help to curb possible predators in areas where the birds are released.

Slow breeders

Birds that reproduce slowly, such as albatrosses (Diomedeidae) and sandhill cranes (*Grus canadensis*), are likely to be highly vulnerable to any changes in

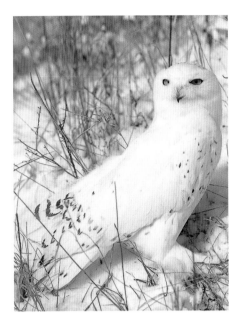

Above: Snowy owls (Nyctea scandiaca) are often seen near coasts outside the breeding season. They are opportunistic hunters, even catching fish on occasion.

their surroundings, whether caused by human interference, climate change, disease, or other factors. Great concern has recently been focused on albatross numbers, which are declining wordwide. Many of these birds have been caught and drowned in fishing nets in recent years. Albatrosses are normally very long-lived and breed very slowly. Any sudden decline in their population is therefore likely to have devastating consequences that cannot easily be reversed.

Below: Sandhill crane (Grus canadensis) with chick. Long-lived, slow-breeding birds such as cranes are the least adaptable when faced with rapid environmental changes of any kind.

green budgies survived to breed and pass on their genes to their descendants, and so green became the dominant color in the feral flocks.

Group living also means that when the flock is feeding and at its most vulnerable, there are extra eyes to watch out for predators and other threats. Within parrot flocks, birds take it in turns to act as sentinels, and screech loudly at any hint of danger.

Effects of humans

It is generally assumed that human interference in the landscape is likely to have harmful effects on avian populations. However, this is not

MIGRATION

Some birds live in a particular place all year round, but many are only temporary visitors. Typically, species fly north into temperate latitudes in spring, and return south at the end of summer. They have a wide distribution, but are seen only in specific parts of their range at certain times of the year.

Many species of birds regularly take long seasonal journeys. The birds that regularly undertake such seasonal movements on specific routes are known as migrants, and the journeys themselves are known as migrations. Many birds migrating from North to South America prefer to fly across Central America rather than the Caribbean. Birds migrate to seek shelter from the elements, to find safe areas to rear their young and, in particular, to seek places where food is plentiful. Birds such as waxwings (Bombycillidae) irrupt to a new location to find food when supplies become scarce in their habitat, but such journeys are less frequent and are irregular. The instinct to migrate dates back millions of years, to a period

Right: This diagram illustrates the main migratory routes in the Americas, where birds fly either down the Central American isthmus, or across the Caribbean via the local islands. In following these traditional routes over or close to land, the birds avoid long and potentially hazardous sea crossings.

Below: The routes taken by birds migrating back and forth to Africa from parts of Europe and western Asia are shown here. Again, crossings are not always made by the most direct route, if this would entail a long and possibly dangerous sea journey.

when the seasons were often much more extreme, which meant that it was difficult to obtain food in a locality throughout the year. This forced birds to move in search of food. Even today, the majority of migratory species live within the world's temperate zones, particularly in the northern hemisphere, where seasonal changes remain pronounced.

Migratory routes

The routes that the birds follow on their journeys are often well defined. Land birds try to avoid flying over large stretches of water, preferring instead to follow coastal routes and crossing the sea at the shortest point. For instance, many birds migrating from Europe to Africa prefer to fly over the Straits of Gibraltar. Frequently

Banding birds

Much of what we know about migration and the lifespan of birds comes from banding studies carried out by ornithologists. Lightweight aluminum bands placed on the birds' legs allow experts to track their movements when the ringed birds are recovered again. Unfortunately, only a very small proportion of ringed birds are ever recovered, so the data gathered is incomplete, but now other methods of tracking, such as radar, are also used to follow the routes taken by flocks of birds, which supplements the information from banding studies.

Below: Banding and collection of "biometric" data from shorebirds in New Jersey. By taking careful measurements of various parts of the body, and weighing the bird as well, scientists are able to build up a physical portrait of various bird populations.

birds fly at much greater altitudes when migrating. Cranes (Gruidae) have been recorded flying at 16,400ft (5,000m) when crossing the mountainous areas in France, and geese (*Anser*) have been observed crossing the Himalayas at altitudes of more than 29,500ft (9,000m). Even if the migratory routes are known, it is often difficult to spot migrating birds because they fly so high.

Speed and distance

Migrating birds also fly at greater speeds than usual, which helps to make their journey time as short as possible. The difference can be significant—migrating swallows (*Hirundo rustica*) travel at speeds between 1.8–8.7mph (3–14km/h) faster than usual, helped by the greater altitude, where the air is thinner and resistance is less.

Some birds travel huge distances on migration. Arctic terns (*Sterna paradisea*), for example, cover distances of more than 9,300 miles (15,000km) in total, as they shuttle between the Arctic and Antarctic. They fly an average distance of 100 miles (160km) every day. Size does not preclude birds from migrating long distances, either. The tiny ruby-throated hummingbird (*Archilochus colubris*) flies over the Gulf of Mexico from the eastern USA every year, a distance of more than 500 miles (800km).

Preparing for migration

The migratory habits of birds have long been the subject of scientific curiosity. As late as the 1800s, it was thought that swallows hibernated in the bottom of ponds because they were seen skimming over the pond surface in groups before disappearing until the following spring. Now we know that they were probably feeding on insects to build up energy supplies for their long journey ahead.

Even today, the precise mechanisms involved in migratory behavior are not fully understood. We do know that birds feed up before setting out on migration, and that various hormonal changes enable them to store more fat

Above: Many birds, like this scarlet tanager (Piranga olivacea) migrate after molting. Damaged plumage can make the task of flying harder and more hazardous.

in their bodies to sustain them on their journey. Feeding opportunities are likely to be more limited than usual when birds are migrating, while their energy requirements are, of course, higher. In addition, birds usually molt just before migrating, so that their plumage is in the best condition to withstand the inevitable buffeting that lies ahead.

Navigation

Birds use both learned and visual cues to orientate themselves when migrating. Young birds of many species, such as swans, learn the route by flying in the company of their elders. However, some young birds set out on their own and reach their destinations successfully without the benefit of experienced companions, navigating by instinct alone. Birds such as swifts (Apopidae) fly mainly during daytime, whereas others, including ducks (Anatidae), migrate at night. Many birds fly direct to their destination, but some may detour and break their journey to obtain food and water before setting out again.

Experiments have shown that birds orientate themselves using the position of the sun and stars, as well as by following familiar landmarks. They also use the Earth's magnetic field to find their position, and thus do not get lost in cloudy or foggy weather, when the sky is obscured. The way in which these various factors come together, however, is not yet fully understood.

BEHAVIOR

Bird behavior, or avian ethology as it is known, is a very broad field. Some patterns of behavior are common to all birds, whereas other actions are very specific, just to a single species or even to an individual population. Interpreting behavior is easier in some cases than in others.

All bird behavior essentially relates to various aspects of survival, such as avoiding predators, obtaining food, finding a mate and breeding successfully. Some behavior patterns are instinctive, while others develop in certain populations of birds as a response to certain conditions. Thus, the way in which birds behave is partly influenced by their environment as well as being largely instinctual.

Age also plays a part in determining behavior, since young birds often behave in a very different way from

Above: An albatross (Diomedeidae) preens the downy plumage of its chick. This helps to cement the bond between them, as well as ensuring that the plumage around the bill does not become matted with food.

adults. Some forms of bird behavior are relatively easy to interpret, while others are a great deal more difficult to explain.

Garden birds
One of the first studies documenting birds' ability to adapt their behavior in response to changes in their environment involved blue tits (*Parus caeruleus*) in Britain. The study showed that certain individuals learned to use their bills to tap through the shiny metallic foil covers on milk bottles to reach the milk. Other blue tits followed their example, and in certain areas householders with milk deliveries had to protect their bottle tops from the birds.

The way in which birds have learned to use various types of garden feeders also demonstrates their ability to modify their existing behavior in response to new conditions when it benefits them. A number of new feeders on the market, designed to thwart squirrels from stealing the food,

exploit birds' ability to adapt in this way. The birds have to squeeze through a small gap to reach the food, just as they might enter the nest. Once one bird has been bold enough to enter in this fashion, others observe and soon follow suit.

Preening
Although preening serves a variety of functions, the most important aspect is keeping the feathers in good condition. It helps to dislodge parasites and removes loose feathers, particularly during molting. It also ensures that the plumage is kept waterproof by spreading oil from the preen gland at the base of the tail.

Preening can be a social activity too. It may be carried out by pairs of males and females during the breeding season, or among a family group.

Aggression
Birds can be surprisingly aggressive toward each other, even to the point of sometimes inflicting fatal injuries. Usually, however, only a few feathers are shed before the weaker individual backs away, without sustaining serious injury. Conflicts of this type can break out over feeding sites or territorial disputes. The risk of aggressive outbreaks is greatest at the start of the breeding season, as this is when the territorial instincts of cock birds are most aroused. Size is no indicator of the potential level of aggression, since some of the smallest birds, such as hummingbirds (Trochilidae) can be ferociously aggressive.

Below: A dispute breaks out between a pair of great-tailed grackles (Quiscalus mexicanus). Such encounters rarely result in serious injury, as the weaker individual usually flies away to escape its rival.

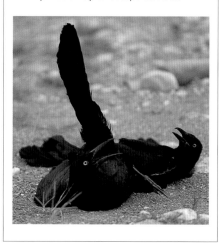

This behavior is seen in a variety of birds, ranging from parrots to finches. Some parrots perform mutual preening throughout the year, which reinforces the pair bond. In some of the Asiatic psittaculid parakeets, however, such as the Alexandrine (*Psittacula eupatria*), the dominant hen allows her mate to preen her only when she is in breeding condition, in which case preening may be seen as a prelude to mating.

Bathing

Preening is not the only way in which birds keep their plumage in good condition. Birds often bathe to remove dirt and debris from their plumage. Small birds wet their feathers by lying on a damp leaf during a shower of rain, in an activity known as leaf-bathing. Other birds immerse themselves in a pool of water, splashing around and ruffling their feathers.

Some birds, especially those found in drier areas of the world, prefer to dust-bathe, lying down in a dusty hollow known as a scrape and using fine earth thrown up by their wings to absorb excess oil from their plumage. Then, by shaking themselves thoroughly, followed by a period of preening, the excess oil is removed.

Sunbathing

Sunbathing may be important in allowing birds to synthesize Vitamin D3 from the ultraviolet rays in sunlight, which is vital for a healthy skeleton. This process can be achieved only by light falling on the bird's skin, which explains why birds ruffle their plumage at this time. Some birds habitually stretch out while sunbathing, while others, such as many pigeons, prefer to rest with one wing

Right: The natural waterproofing present on the plumage ensures that birds do not become saturated when swimming or caught in a shower of rain. This would destroy the warm layer of air surrounding the body created by the down feathering, and leave them vulnerable to hypothermia. Nevertheless birds do need to dry their plumage, which is what this American anhinga (Anhinga anhinga) is doing, with its wings outstretched.

raised, leaning over at a strange angle on the perch. Vasa parrots (*Coracopsis*), found on the island of Madagascar, frequently behave in this fashion, although sunbathing is generally not common in this group of birds.

Maintaining health

Some people believe that when birds are ill, they eat particular plants that have medicinal properties, but this theory is very difficult to prove. One form of behavior that does confer health benefits has been documented, however: it involves the use of ants. Instead of eating these insects, some birds occasionally rub them in among their feathers. This causes the ants to release formic acid, which acts as a potent insecticide, killing off lurking parasites such as mites and lice. Blue jays (*Cyanocitta cristata*) and also starlings (Sturnidae) and Eurasian blackbirds (*Turdus merula*) are among the species that have been observed using insects in this way. Members of the crow family have also been seen perching on smoking chimney pots or above bonfires, ruffling their feathers and allowing the smoke to penetrate their plumage. The smoke is thought to kill off parasites in a process that confers the same benefits as anting.

Above: Birds such as the cattle egret (Bubulcus ibis) form unusual associations with large mammals. They will mingle among herds as they feed, keeping a sharp watch for potential prey such as invertebrates, or other creatures, that may be flushed from the grass by the mammals as they move.

Below: A Gila woodpecker (Melanerpes uropygialis) feeding on cactus fruit. These desert-dwelling woodpeckers will also bore into larger cacti to create their nest site.

BIRDWATCHING

Thanks to their widespread distribution, birds can be seen in virtually any locality, even in the center of cities. You don't need any special equipment to watch birds, but a pair of binoculars will help you to gain a better insight into avian behavior, by allowing you to study birds at close range.

Birdwatching can be carried out almost anywhere around the world. Many people enjoy simply watching the birds that visit their garden. A greater variety of species can be seen if the birdwatcher ventures further afield, to local parks, woods or wetlands for example. Birdwatching vacations and sponsored birdwatching competitions offer opportunities to see an even greater variety of birds in different localities. Seasonal changes in bird populations mean that even if you visit the same area through the year, you will see new species at different times.

Above: At many major reserves where birds congregate, special permanent birdwatching hides have been set up to give visitors a good view without disturbing the birds themselves.

Drawing birds for reference

1. Sketching birds is relatively straight-forward if you follow this procedure. Start by drawing an egg shape for the body, with a smaller egg above, which will become the head, and another to form the rump. A center line through the head circle will form the basis for the bill. Now add circles and lines to indicate the position of the wings and tail. Add lines for the legs and then sketch in the feet and claws.

2. Use an indelible fine-line felt-tip pen to ink in the shape of the bird that you have drawn previously in pencil, avoiding the unwanted construction lines.

3. Colored pencils will allow you to add more detail after you have rubbed out any unwanted pencil markings.

4. If you take a number of prepared head shapes with you into the field, you can fill in the detail quickly and easily, enabling you to identify birds later.

Getting a good view

Binoculars can be purchased from camera stores and similar outlets, but it is important to test them before deciding which model to buy, particularly as they vary quite significantly in price. When purchasing binoculars, you will need to consider not only the power of magnification, but also how closely the binoculars can be focused, particularly if you going to use them at home, where the bird table is likely to be relatively close.

Binoculars vary according to their power of magnification and the length of the objective lens in millimeters, with the lens modifying the image. The lens' length and magnification are given in the specifications: binoculars described as 8x45 multiply the image by eight compared with how it would appear to the naked eye and have an objective lens of 45mm, which is important in determining the focus.

Two important considerations stem from the power of magnification. First, the depth of field is important, since it affects the area of the image that is in focus. The greater the magnification, the shallower the depth of field. A deep depth of field can be helpful, since it ensures that a larger proportion of the birds on view are in focus, which avoids the need to refocus constantly. If the depth of field is shallow, only the birds in the center will be in focus. Second, the degree of magnification also affects the field of vision—the area that you can see through the binoculars. A wide field of vision will help you to locate birds more easily.

Buying binoculars

A number of other factors may be considered when buying binoculars.
• Weight is important. Consider buying a lightweight pair if you intend using binoculars for long periods. They should also feel balanced in the hands.
• For people with large hands, small binoculars may be hard to adjust and not very comfortable to hold. Pay attention to the focusing mechanism—it should be easy to operate.
• Try the eyecups of the binoculars to see how comfortable they feel. If you wear glasses, it is important that the cups give you a full field of vision. Binoculars with adjustable eyecups are better for people who wear glasses.
• Is the design of good quality? It could be worthwhile paying extra for waterproofing. The better-quality

Below: A view of a hide. External camouflage, easy access and good viewing positions are essential features in the design of such units. Even so, it may take birds some time to accept the presence of a hide.

Above: A backyard bird table will attract many species to feed, like this starling (Sturnus vulgaris). If it is carefully sited, you should be able to see the birds from inside your home.

Right: Hanging feeders are increasingly popular in American backyards as a means of encouraging birds to visit. The positioning of this orange makes it easily accessible to this hungry Baltimore oriole (Icterus galbula), and other fruit-eating species, providing them with a vertical grip as well as a source of food.

models have their chambers filled with nitrogen gas to prevent any condensation developing.
• The design should be sturdy, with a solid protective casing.

Fieldscopes

Apart from binoculars, dedicated bird-watchers often use birding telescopes, called fieldscopes. These are ideal for use in hides as they can be mounted in various ways, using either a bench clamp fitting or a tripod. Fieldscopes are equipped with lenses similar to those in binoculars, but are more suited to long-term use, when you are watching a nest for example, as you do not have to keep holding the scope while waiting for a bird to return. Instead, attach the scope to a branch or bench and train it on the nest, then simply be patient until you see the bird return.

Making notes

When observing birds either in the garden or further afield, it is always useful to have a notebook handy to write down details and make sketches.

When sketching, proceed from a few quick pencil lines to a more finished portrait as time allows. Water-soluble pencils are helpful for coloring sketches, as the colors can be spread using water and a small paintbrush. If you spot a bird you cannot identify, jot down the details quickly in your notebook. Note the bird's colors and markings. Notice the length of the neck and legs, and the shape of its bill. Assess the bird's size in relation to familiar species, and try to decide which family you think it belongs to. Your notes can then be compared with a field guide or other sources of information to identify the bird.

FIELDCRAFT

If you are seriously interested in birdwatching, you will need to develop fieldcraft skills. There is a significant difference between watching birds casually in a garden and tracking down particular species in remote areas, where preparation is important. Don't neglect your own safety in the wild.

Left: Hand-held binoculars or a viewing scope attached to a tripod can help you to study both common and rare species. Taking notes is useful, especially if you intend to write up details of your observations.

Photography

In the past, birdwatchers relied on 35mm SLR cameras and telephoto lenses to record their sightings. Today, however, birders are increasingly using digital cameras. These work very well when combined via a connector to a viewing scope that magnifies the image, like a telephoto lens. Digital cameras have the further advantage that they do not require film, but store images in their memory. Unwanted pictures can simply be deleted, while the best images can be transferred to a computer and printed out. Although you will not run out of film, digital cameras do use a surprising amount of power, so remember to take spare

Research and careful preparation are vital to the success of any field trip. You should also select clothing and equipment suited to the particular place where you intend to study birds.

Clothing and equipment

Suitable clothing is vital to keep you warm and dry when birdwatching. Waterproof footwear will be needed when visiting wetlands, or after rain. Dull-colored clothing will allow you to blend in with the landscape so you can approach the birds more closely. A camping mat can be useful if you intend spending time on the ground.

In addition to packing your binoculars, camera equipment and perhaps a viewing scope, you may also want to take a notebook or sketchpad. A field guide will help to identify birds, while a waterproof knapsack will protect all your belongings.

Preparation

It always helps to do your homework before setting out. Investigating the habits of the birds you hope to see will help you to decide on the best place to go, and the time of day when they are

most likely to be seen. It may be useful to draw up a checklist highlighting key features of the species concerned in advance. You can then refer to these in the field. Studying a local map prior to your visit will help you to orient yourself in new surroundings. Good preparation is especially important in areas where you are likely to be unfamiliar with the birds concerned.

Below: Plumage details, such as the handsome markings of this blue jay (Cyanocitta cristata), may be captured using a conventional camera with a telephoto lens, or using a digital camera or camcorder linked to a viewing scope.

batteries with you on field trips. Digital camcorders can also be linked with viewing scopes, and are more flexible than cameras. Not only does a camcorder enable you to record the bird's song—which can be significant, especially if there is any doubt about identification—but you can also obtain a sequence of still images, especially if you can see the bird from different angles. Flight patterns can be recorded in this way, which again can help with identification. Even in relatively dark surroundings, some camcorders will function well.

Using hides and cover

On recognized reserves, there are likely to be hides in the best localities for birdwatching. Hides allow you to observe birds at relatively close quarters, and also offer excellent opportunities to photograph or film birds in their natural habitat. Even so, patience is likely to be needed for successful birding, as there will be no guarantees that you will see the species you hope to spot.

In areas where no hide is available, take cover behind shrubs, tree trunks or raised banks, or even in a parked car. Birds are highly attuned to the

slightest hint of danger, such as humans approaching. In areas where no cover is available, stand, kneel or lie in a comfortable position and try to move as little as possible. When approaching birds, make sure your position is downwind, so the sounds of your approach don't frighten them away.

Seeking rarities

Birdwatching magazines can be useful in identifying sites where rarities have been spotted. For up-to-the-minute news, you will need to seek out either a regularly updated website or an information phone line giving details of the latest sightings. Birders with access to email can also receive

Above: In some areas, there may not be any natural cover or hides available. To get close to birds, you will need to dress inconspicuously so that you blend into the background, and try to keep as still as you possibly can. Birdwatching requires plenty of patience.

bulletins listing where particular rarities have cropped up. These are most likely to be recorded after bad weather such as fierce storms which can blow migrant birds off-course.

Bear in mind that many people will be drawn to a place where an unusual species has been sighted, and it is important not to create a disturbance or to trespass on private land. Similarly, it is a criminal offence in some areas to disturb breeding birds. Always act in a responsible manner when birdwatching.

Getting the best results

• Plan well beforehand, including checking tide times if relevant. Tidal areas can be particularly hazardous where there is quicksand.
• Remember that bird populations may vary according to the time of year.
• Never neglect your own safety. Let someone else know where you are going, and when you intend to return.
• Check the weather forecast first, and take a cell phone in case you get into difficulties.
• Take a local map and also a compass to guide you if you get lost. Allow enough time to locate and then observe the birds.

Below: There are now many organized trips taking keen birders to exotic localities, such as this tour of La Selva Biological Station, the center for rainforest research, in Costa Rica.

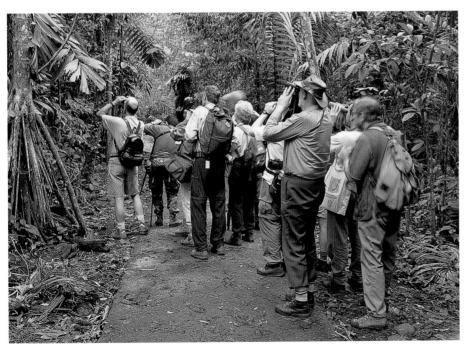

ZONES AND HABITATS

Birds have been exceedingly successful in colonizing the planet. Their warm-blooded nature and ability to fly have helped them to reach and then adapt to life in some of the world's most inaccessible places. They are found naturally on all continents, even successfully inhabiting Antarctica.

Zoologists divide the world into broad geographical zones, within which there are many different habitats. This approach reflects the movements of the Earth's landmasses through geological time, and so helps to show relationships between species occurring in various parts of the world today.

The Americas

In the distant past, North America was separated from its southern neighbor, and they had different origins. North America was originally attached to what is now Europe and later drifted westwards, while South America was once joined to a huge southern landmass that geologists call Gondwana, which included what is now the Indian subcontinent, Australia, Africa and Antarctica. South America split off at an earlier stage in

geological history than did North America—more than 100 million years ago—at a time when dinosaurs were in the ascendancy and the skies were occupied by flying reptiles called pterosaurs, rather than birds.

When birds began to evolve on this southern continent, they did so in isolation from the rest of the world. For this reason, the bird life that occurs today in this southern zone is known as neotropical, to distinguish it from that found in North America, which is known as nearctic. Later the avian populations of the Nearctic and Neotropical zones mingled somewhat by way of the Central American land bridge that was created when these two vast landmasses joined. However, unique forms still exist that are found only in South America, reflecting their isolated development in prehistory.

Above: This map shows how the different continents are believed to have formed and divided, giving rise to the familiar continents that we know today (see map below). These continental movements have, in turn, had a direct impact on the distribution of birds today.

Above: Some birds can be seen far outside their natural range, thanks to human intervention. Escapes from aviaries by, and deliberate releases of, orange bishops (Euplectes orix), normally found in Africa, have led to the recent establishment of this species in Los Angeles and Phoenix, Arizona.

The Palaearctic

Europe has been separated from North America by the Atlantic Ocean for more than 50 million years, but the bird species of these now separate areas still show some evidence of their common past. In prehistory, Europe formed, and still forms, part of a much broader area known as the Palaearctic realm, which extends right across the northern continent from Iceland eastward to Japan. Fossilized remains suggest that this region was the cradle of avian evolution, where the first members of the group probably originated more than 80 million years ago. Most zoologists believe that the oldest-known bird, *Archaeopteryx*, was not in fact the first of the avian line, but as yet its immediate ancestors have not been discovered.

The distribution of avian species in the northern hemisphere has been affected in the more recent geological past by the spread and subsequent retreat of the ice sheets from the far north. Today, Europe and Asia experience a climate similar to that of the corresponding area of North America, ranging from arctic to subtropical according to latitude. The two regions even have some birds in common, especially in the far north, where certain species have a circum-polar distribution—they are found right around the polar region.

Africa, southern Asia and Australasia

As part of the great southern continent of Gondwana, Africa used to be attached to South America, but subsequently remained in contact with what is now the Indian subcontinent during the critical early phase in avian evolution, approximately 60 million years ago. This distant history is reflected even today by the large number of avian species found south of what has become the Sahara Desert. This zone is now described as the Ethiopian realm, although it covers virtually all of Africa.

The Indian subcontinent became a separate landmass when Gondwana broke up. It ultimately drifted north, colliding and eventually joining with what is now the Asian landmass, and creating the Himalayan mountains in the process. As in Africa, the broadly tropical climate and the landscape have altered little since then, which has meant that a number of the species that evolved here are found nowhere else in the world.

East and south of India lie the islands that comprise the Australasian realm, which includes Australia, New Guinea and New Zealand. These islands once formed part of the vast landmass of Gondwana, but later broke away and have been isolated from the rest of the world for millions of years. A diversity of bird species found nowhere else in the world can be seen here as a result.

Present distribution

Birds' current distribution throughout the world is affected by a number of different factors, as well as the history of their evolution. The ability to fly has allowed birds to become very widely distributed, as has their warm-blooded nature, which has meant that they are far less vulnerable to climatic factors than cold-blooded creatures. Lifestyle, and particularly the range of foods that are available, also play a part. As a result of all these factors, birdwatchers know that they are more likely to encounter certain groups of birds in specific types of habitat. The major, and richly diverse, avian habitats of the American world are listed on the pages that follow.

Below: Common, or European, starlings (Sturnus vulgaris) are now well established outside their natural range. This picture was taken in the USA where, during the 1800s, the species was introduced. It has since spread widely across North America, and can also be found in Australia, and other localities.

THE OCEANS

The world's oceans provide a very rich source of food for all birds able to exploit it. Fish and invertebrates such as squid and krill form the basis of the diet of seabirds, some of which range extensively across the world's oceans and are frequently sighted long distances from land.

The huge expanse of the oceans, and the difficulty of observing seabirds, means that relatively little is known about many species. This lack of knowledge was confirmed by the case of the Bermuda petrel (*Pterodroma cahow*). This species was believed to have become extinct during the 1600s, but, remarkably, a surviving population was rediscovered in 1951 after more than three hundred years. Seabirds survive out at sea with the help of special salt-excreting glands in

the nasal area (just above their bills) that allow them to drink seawater without getting dehydrated.

Breeding habits

Many seabirds are social by nature, forming huge breeding colonies on rocky outcrops by the sea. Indeed, one of the main factors restricting seabird populations can be the lack of nesting sites. By congregating in large colonies the birds can maximize their reproductive success while reducing the effects of predators on their numbers. Nest-raiders such as greater black-backed gulls (*Larus marinus*) may be unable to inflict damage on a breeding colony if the birds are so densely packed that the raiders cannot land.

Feeding

The feeding habits of seabirds have a significant impact on their lifestyle. Albatrosses (Diomedeidae), for example, spend most of their lives flying above the oceans. Their large wingspan allows them to glide almost effortlessly for long periods, swooping down to take food from the surface or even catching flying fish above the waves, rather than entering the water. Other species, such as gannets (Sulidae), dive beneath the surface to feed.

Above: Some seabirds spend their entire lives on the water, and will not venture any great distance from this habitat. Others, such as these knots (Calidris canutus), are only in the ocean for part of the year. They retreat inland during the breeding season, to nest in the far north on frozen tundra.

Below: Not all seabirds feed on fish. This white-vented storm petrel (Oceanites gracilis) is feeding on planktonic debris, while paddling with its feet on the surface of the water.

Right: The ocean can be a hostile environment, with rough weather sometimes making feeding conditions difficult. High winds can batter birds and blow them off course, while oil spillages have presented a new threat in recent times. Ultimately, all seabirds are forced onto land to reproduce. Many species seek out remote oceanic islands to do so. There they can breed without being harassed by people or encountering introduced predators such as domestic cats.

Birdwatching tips

• Seabirds such as albatrosses are attracted to passing ships because of the food that is thrown overboard. This means they are relatively easy to locate in certain areas—for example near shipping lanes.
• Ornithologists can often take trips on local boats to view seabird colonies. These and other ocean crossings may present a good opportunity to watch birds feeding out at sea.
• If you are prone to seasickness, don't forget to take medication beforehand if you think you may feel ill on a trip.
• Binoculars can easily be lost overboard from a small boat in choppy oceans. Always sling them (and any camera equipment) around your neck, rather than simply holding them in your hands.

Typical sightings in seas and oceans, depending to some extent on location:
• Auks
• Gannets
• Albatrosses
• Petrels

Below: For most ornithologists, organized charter boat trips present the only way to reach seabird colonies.

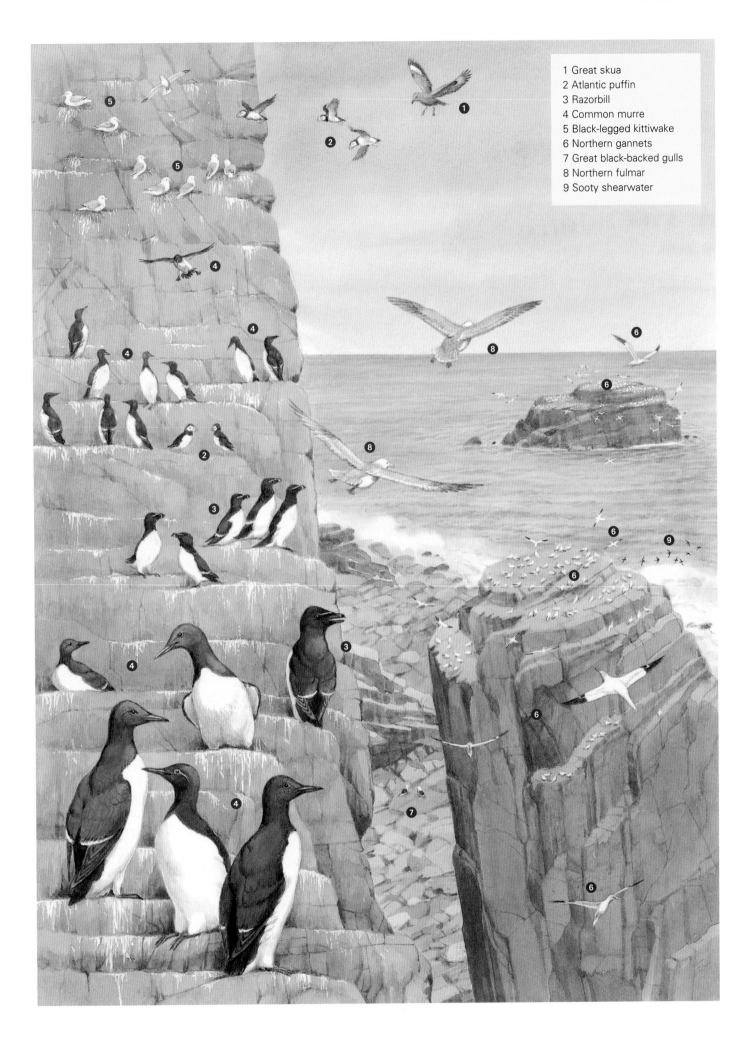

1 Great skua
2 Atlantic puffin
3 Razorbill
4 Common murre
5 Black-legged kittiwake
6 Northern gannets
7 Great black-backed gulls
8 Northern fulmar
9 Sooty shearwater

SEASHORE AND ESTUARY

Tidal rhythms have a significant impact on the habits of birds found on seashores and estuaries. These birds usually group together to feed on mudflats and sandbars that are uncovered at low tide. As the incoming tide encroaches, the birds are forced to retreat to the shoreline.

Gulls typify the image of the seashore more than any other group of birds, being a familiar sight on coasts the world over. These adaptable birds also venture well inland, especially to locations where food is available, such as public parks with ponds and even the less salubrious surroundings of refuse dumps.

Above: Sanderlings (Calidris alba) *demonstrate the features of a typical wader. The daily lives of such birds are directly influenced by the movements of the tide.*

Below: It is very difficult to get close to seabirds such as these terns, as they tend to be wary and may take flight. It is therefore better to pick a well-concealed vantage point and wait for the birds to approach.

Lifestyle and feeding

Wading birds that frequent seashores typically have relatively long legs compared with perching birds, which enable them to walk through shallow water. Their narrow bills allow them to probe for invertebrates concealed in the mud. Some waders have evolved more specialized feeding habits, which are reflected in the shape of their bills. The American oystercatcher (*Haematopus palliatus*), for example, has a chisel-like tip to its bill that allows it to split open mollusk shells.

Shorebirds feed on a range of creatures, and can therefore be sighted further inland, even if only seeking sanctuary from storms. Some shorebirds are migratory, spending summer as far north as the Arctic Circle before heading south for winter again.

Breeding habits

Many birds that live close to the shoreline have to breed in the open. The eggs and chicks of such species,

which include curlews *(Numenius)*, have markings that conceal them well among the sand or pebbles. This cryptic coloration also plays a part in adulthood, with typical shades of gray, brown and white plumage merging into the background of the shoreline.

Within the tropics, a number of shorebirds have adapted to living in coastal mangrove forests, the roots of which are submerged by the incoming tide. They include some of the most spectacular members of the group, such as the scarlet ibis (*Eudocimus ruber*). These birds use the mangroves for roosting and breeding because they can nest off the ground there.

Right: The day-to-day distribution of seashore and estuarine birds is likely to be influenced by the weather. If conditions are stormy, birds often retreat to estuaries and coastal lagoons; in icy winter weather, a variety of unexpected species may be seen at estuaries, since these stretches of water do not freeze over, unlike surrounding areas of fresh water such as lakes and rivers.

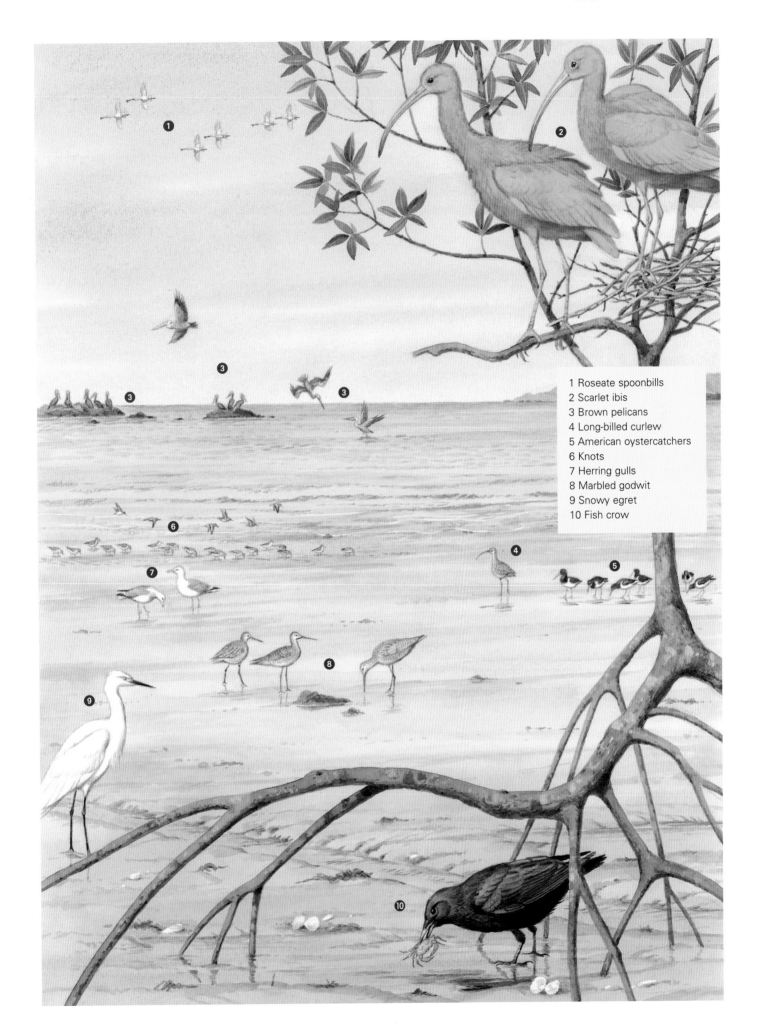

1 Roseate spoonbills
2 Scarlet ibis
3 Brown pelicans
4 Long-billed curlew
5 American oystercatchers
6 Knots
7 Herring gulls
8 Marbled godwit
9 Snowy egret
10 Fish crow

FRESHWATER LAKES, PONDS AND RIVERS

The speed of the water flow in freshwater habitats has a direct impact on the vegetation that grows there, which in turn influences the types of birds that may be seen. Some birds are drawn to lakes, ponds and rivers mainly for food, whereas others seek sanctuary from would-be predators there.

A wide variety of birds can be encountered by lakes, ponds and rivers, but not all are easy to observe. In areas of slow-flowing or still, shallow water where reed beds are well established, rails of various types (Rallidae) are often present, but these birds are shy by nature. Their mottled plumage provides camouflage, while their slim, tall body shape coupled with long, narrow toes allows them to move quietly through the vegetation.

Finding food

Many birds of prey hunt in freshwater habitats, swooping low over the water to seize fish by day and even at night. Ospreys (*Pandion haliaetus*) have very powerful, hooked talons, allowing them to hold onto slippery fish that they lift out of the water during flight. Other hunters rely on different tactics to catch food. Herons (Ardeidae) wait in the shallows and seize fish that swim in range of their sharp, powerful bills. Some fish-eating birds such as kingfishers (Alcedinidae) dive to seize their prey, which they may feed to their young in river bank nests.

Nesting

Some birds are drawn to lakes and rivers not so much by food but by nesting opportunities. Swallows (*Hirundo rustica*) collect damp mud from the

Above: A sharp bill, narrow head and powerful neck mean that birds such as the red-necked grebe (Podiceps grisegena) are well equipped to seize aquatic prey.

water's edge to make their nests, and may also catch midges flying above the water. Most birds that actually nest by ponds and rivers seek seclusion when breeding. They hide their nest away, or make it hard to reach by choosing a spot surrounded by water, while taking care to avoid sites that may flood. Trumpeter swans (*Cygnus buccinator*) construct large nests, which restricts their choice of sites. Both sexes, but especially the cob (male), defend the nest ferociously. These largish birds are capable of inflicting painful, damaging

blows with their wings on would-be wild predators, dogs or even people who venture too close.

Birdwatching tips
• Patience is essential when watching freshwater birds, as many species are shy and easily frightened away.
• Certain localities, such as large lakes and gravel pits, are particularly good for spotting waterfowl in winter. Check local details in field guides or on websites.
• Quietly paddling a canoe up a river can be a good way to spot birds, but plan carefully and be alert to possible dangers, such as strong currents, weirs or waterfalls on the route.
• Take great care near rivers when there is a risk of flooding, such as after heavy rain.

Typical sightings by lakes, ponds and rivers, depending on location:
• Ducks, geese and swans
• Rails
• Herons
• Birds of prey

Below: The keen eyesight and long legs of birds such as the great blue heron (Ardea herodias) help them to hunt effectively in freshwater habitats.

Below: A wattled jacana (Jacana jacana), photographed here in Trinidad, has long toes which support its weight when walking across lily pads, and prevent it from sinking down.

Right: Reedbeds associated with freshwater habitats provide cover for many species of birds. The dense vegetation in such areas means that birdwatching can be difficult. The narrow body shape and agility of many freshwater birds allow them to move easily through dense vegetation, avoiding detection. Fortunately, birds swimming into open water will be much easier to spot.

1 Whistling swans
2 Belted kingfisher
3 Yellow-headed blackbird
4 Osprey
5 Common loon
6 Lesser scaup
7 Canvasback
8 Wood duck family
9 Green heron
10 King rail
11 Great blue heron

TEMPERATE WOODLAND

The temperate woodlands of the Northern Hemisphere have altered significantly over time owing to climate change, receding in cold periods and expanding in warmer eras. Coniferous forests extend north to the treeless area known as the tundra, where it is too cold for even hardy trees to grow.

Bird life in coniferous forests is less varied than in deciduous, broad-leaved woodlands, largely because there are fewer feeding opportunities. Nonetheless some species manage to thrive in this cooler habitat.

Coniferous woodlands

Clark's nutcracker (*Nucifraga columbiana*) of the North American forests is one such success. Their curving bills allow these specialized members of the crow family to extract the seeds from pine cones effectively.

The food supply in this habitat is not guaranteed, however. There are barren years when the trees do not produce as many cones as usual, forcing the birds to abandon their regular haunts and fly elsewhere. These unpredictable movements, known as irruptions, occur when birds suddenly appear in large numbers outside their normal range, searching for alternative sources of food. They later disappear

Below: Some predatory birds have adapted to life in temperate forests, especially owls such as this large-eared owl (Asio otis). These hunters depend largely on rodents for food.

Above: Some birds, like this wild turkey, (Meleagris gallopavo), nest on the ground, concealing their presence from other creatures as much as possible. The chicks are able to move immediately after hatching.

just as suddenly as they arrived, and may not return again for years. In northerly areas the landscape is covered in snow for much of the winter. Some species, including various corvids and woodpeckers, prepare for the cold weather by burying stores of nuts or hiding them in trees.

Owls are frequently found in coniferous forests, preying on the rodents that can be quite plentiful there. However, owls may also be forced to hunt elsewhere if the numbers of their prey plummet, as occasionally happens when there is a shortage of pine cones.

Deciduous woodlands

A greater variety of feeding opportunities exists for birds in deciduous forests. Such woodland is more open, which means that there is a significant understorey of vegetation and insects are more plentiful. Migratory birds take advantage of the feeding opportunities in these forests in summer. Ground birds of various types, including wild turkeys (*Meleagris gallopavo*), are also found here. During the breeding season they congregate in forest clearings to display and mate. These birds eat a

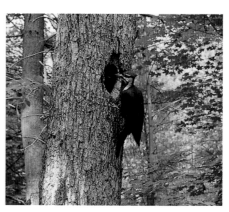

Above: A pileated woodpecker (Dryocopus pileatus) male returns to the nest site. Trees provide relatively safe nesting havens, especially for birds such as woodpeckers that can create their own nesting holes.

variety of foods, ranging from seeds to berries and invertebrates, depending on the time of year.

Birdwatching tips

• Spring is a good time to spot birds in deciduous woodlands, before the trees are covered in leaves.
• Woodlands and particularly coniferous forests can be disorientating, so take a map and compass if you're going any distance in case you lose your bearings.
• In summer, woodland glades attract invertebrates, which in turn attract insectivorous birds in search of prey.
• Stand quietly in woodlands and listen— the song of woodland birds helps to reveal their presence.

Typical sightings in temperate woodlands, depending to some extent on location:
• Woodpeckers
• Finches
• Owls
• Warblers

Right: In many ways, temperate woodland is an ideal avian habitat during the warm months of the year, providing a wide range of food, excellent cover and a variety of nesting sites. During the winter months, however, life here can become much harsher. Once the leaves have fallen, the birds will be much more conspicuous, and food is likely to be harder to find. Survival will become even more difficult if snow blankets the ground.

1 Black-capped chickadee
2 Goshawk
3 Pileated woodpecker
4 Winter wren
5 Hermit thrush
6 Yellow warbler
7 Long-eared owl
8 Pine siskins
9 White-breasted nuthatch

TROPICAL RAINFOREST

Over long periods, tropical rainforests have provided relatively stable environments compared with temperate forests, and are home to some spectacular species. Unfortunately, many tracts of forest are not easily accessible. Choose locations carefully to maximize your chance of seeing a wide range of birds.

Many of the birds inhabiting rainforest areas are brightly colored, but their vibrant plumage is very effectively concealed in this dark, shadowy environment. Only flashes of color may be seen as the plumage is lit by shafts of sunlight penetrating through the dense canopy of the forest.

Rainforest diversity

The stable environment of the rainforest has undoubtedly contributed to the diversity of bird life found there. Fruit is especially plentiful, and specialist fruit-eating birds, known as frugivores, are therefore numerous. Their presence is essential to the long-term well-being of the rainforest, as they help to distribute the seeds of the fruits on which they feed. The seeds are excreted in their droppings, often some distance away from where the fruit was originally eaten. This method of seed dispersal helps to ensure the continued regeneration of the forest.

Birds of prey can also be observed in tropical rainforests, having adapted well to forest life, and there are even a

Below: A yellow-naped Amazon (Amazona ochrocephala) feeding. The unchanging climatic conditions in rainforests mean that food is readily available here through the year.

number of species that specialize in hunting other birds. These predators are relatively few in number, however, compared with the overall numbers of birds found in this habitat.

Many rainforest species have localized distributions. Although some toucans, for example, may have extensive ranges, the distribution of some of Hawaii's native birds may be confined to just a single island. Vast tracts of the world's rainforests are still so remote and inaccessible that even today, particularly on the South American continent, new species of birds are still regularly being discovered by explorers each year.

Threatened habitat

It is well known that the world's rainforests are being felled alarmingly quickly. The fast rate of destruction means that it is possible that some species may become extinct before they have even been identified. Museum collections around the world contain various hummingbirds (Trochilidae) and tanagers (Thraupidae), for example, that are known only from single specimens. The birds' distributions are unrecorded and nothing more has been documented about them.

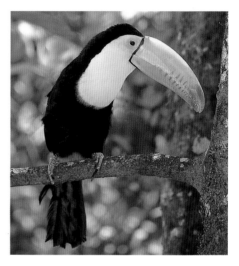

Above: Toucans are among the most distinctive of all birds found in tropical rainforests. Their large but lightweight bills assist them in reaching fruits that would otherwise be inaccessible.

Birdwatching tips
• Rainforests are potentially dangerous places, so go with an experienced guide or group, and don't be tempted to wander off into the forest on your own.
• You are often more likely to hear rather than see birds in this leafy environment.
• Pausing quietly for a time should allow you to spot bird life more easily.
• Photography is often difficult in the forest because of the low light.
• The high humidity, almost daily rainfall and biting insects in rainforests can create additional problems.

Typical sightings in tropical rainforests, depending to some extent on location:
• Parrots
• Barbets
• Cotingas
• Trogons

Right: The dense upper canopy of the rainforest provides both a screen and a vantage point for birds, depending on their lifestyle. Hunters may perch among the tallest trees or fly over the canopy, seeking signs of possible prey beneath, while nearer to the ground, nectar-eating birds seek flowers to feed from. Fruit is also abundant in these lush forests, so frugivorous species are commonly encountered here too.

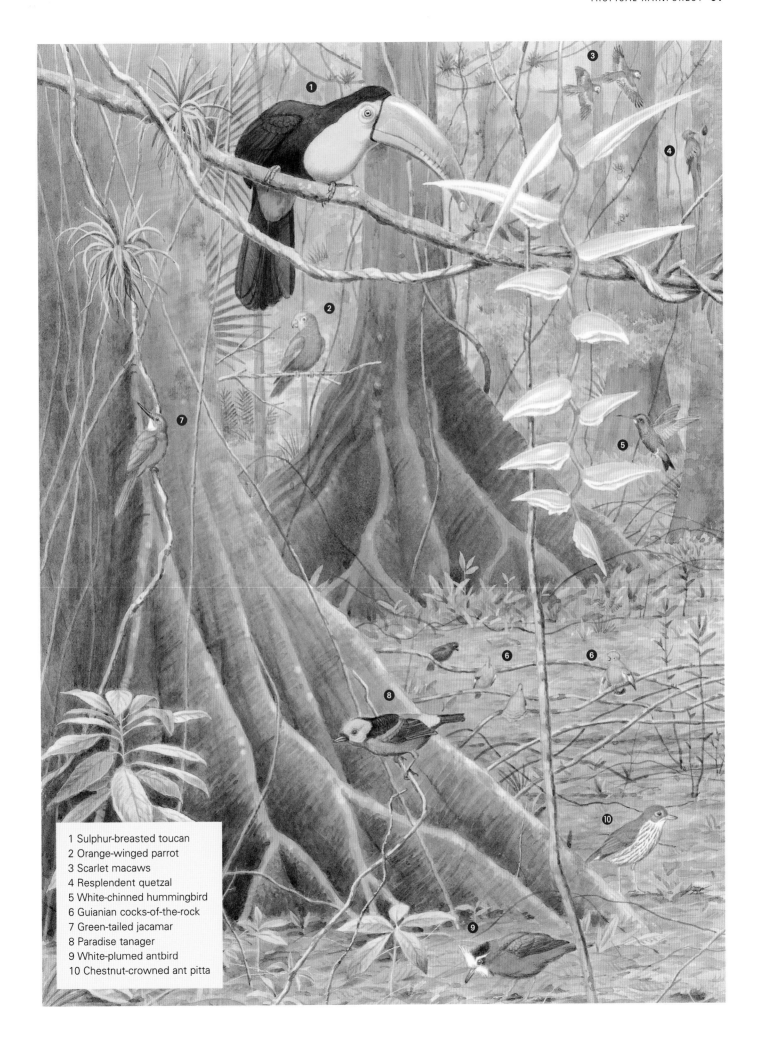

1 Sulphur-breasted toucan
2 Orange-winged parrot
3 Scarlet macaws
4 Resplendent quetzal
5 White-chinned hummingbird
6 Guianian cocks-of-the-rock
7 Green-tailed jacamar
8 Paradise tanager
9 White-plumed antbird
10 Chestnut-crowned ant pitta

TUNDRA AND POLAR REGIONS

Birds have successfully colonized many harsh environments, including the treeless tundra and freezing Antarctic. A surprisingly wide range of birds may be sighted on the tundra, especially in summer, when many migratory birds arrive to breed.

The treeless lands of the far north are inhospitable in winter, so many birds visit only for the summer. Icy Antarctica is even harsher, yet birds such as penguins are year-round residents on coastlines.

Antarctic survivors

As the huge landmass of Antarctica drifted gradually southward millions of years ago, so the seabirds there adapted their lifestyle to survive the harshest conditions on Earth. The freezing cold and biting winds combine to create a numbing wind-chill factor that few creatures could survive, but penguins have adapted to thrive in this habitat. The lack of nesting material and the threat of fatal chilling if the eggs or young are exposed to the elements for even a few seconds have affected their breeding habits. Emperor penguins (*Aptenodytes forsteri*) lay only a single egg, which is kept wedged between the top of their flippered feet

Above: Unlike many birds from the far north, the white plumage of these snow geese (Anser caerulescans) remains the same color throughout the year. There is, however, a much rarer pale blue form of the plumage.

and their abdomen. Emperors have an increased number of blood vessels here, to convey heat to the developing embryo through the eggshell.

Penguins have in fact reversed the general evolutionary path of birds to survive in this harsh environment. In the course of millions of years, most birds evolved increasingly lightweight bodies to facilitate flight, but the body weight of penguins increased because of a build-up of the subcutaneous fat that helps to insulate them against the bitter cold. The evolution of their

Below: Antarctic seabirds such as the cape petrel (Daption capense) benefit from the rich food supply in the southern oceans. These birds fly north to escape the worst winter weather, and only return to the shores of Antarctica during the brief summer to nest.

wings into flippers and their streamlined shape combine to make them highly effective marine predators.

The northern tundra

In the far north, the treeless tundra landscape is transformed during the brief summer months when the snow melts. The topsoil thaws too, and the ground becomes boggy because the melt water cannot drain away through the permanently frozen layer beneath. Instead, water forms shallow pools at the surface, where mosquitoes and other insects breed in large numbers. These invertebrates and other food attract a variety of birds as temporary visitors. The migrants nest and quickly rear their young before the weather turns cold and they head south again.

Right: Many birds found in areas where snow often blankets the ground and there is little natural cover have mainly white plumage. This is true of both predators such as snowy owls (Nyctea scandiaca) and also prey. Other adaptations that assist survival in cold habitats include extra feathering over the body extending to the feet, and greater reserves of body fat.

Birdwatching tips

• Wear pale or dull-colored clothing to conceal your presence in these cold, treeless areas where there is little natural cover. Of course, all clothing must be warm as well.

• Take mosquito repellent when visiting the tundra during the summer.

• Allow for the bright light when photographing in snowy landscapes. Glare reflecting off the snow may distort your camera's light readings, so you may need to compensate.

• An increasing number of ornithological trips to the Antarctic allow you to visit this part of the world accompanied by experienced guides.

Typical sightings in tundra or polar landscapes, depending on your location in the Northern or Southern Hemisphere:

• Waterfowl
• Snowy owls
• Waders
• Penguins

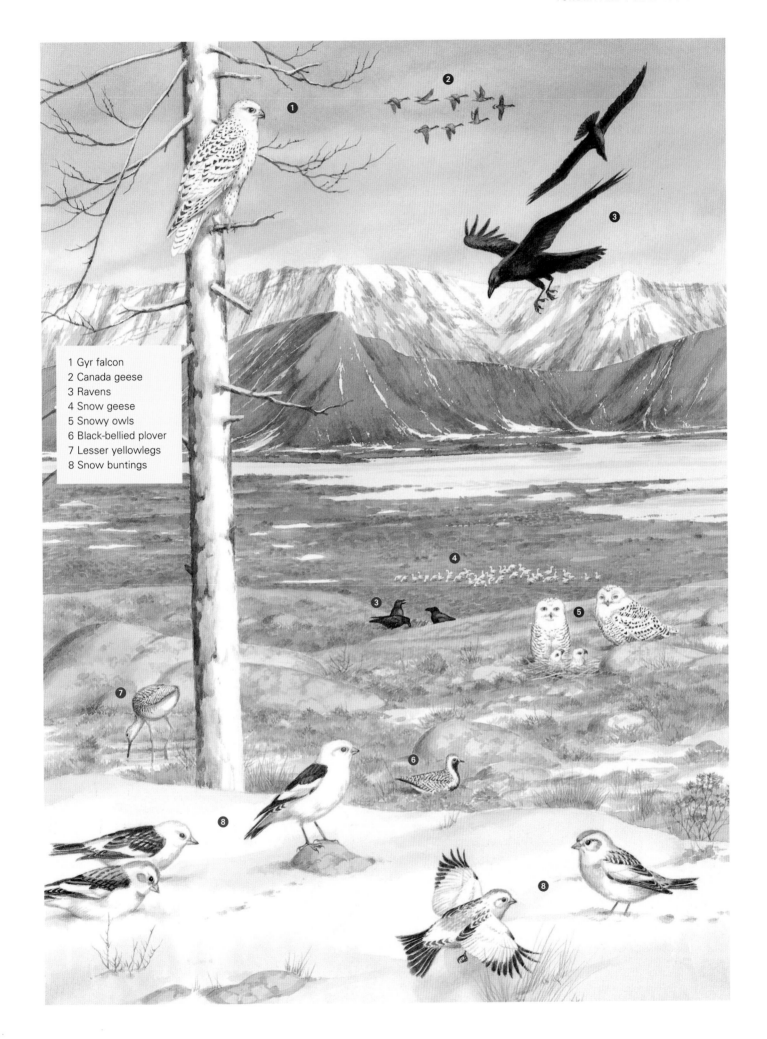

1 Gyr falcon
2 Canada geese
3 Ravens
4 Snow geese
5 Snowy owls
6 Black-bellied plover
7 Lesser yellowlegs
8 Snow buntings

GRASSLAND, STEPPE AND MOORLAND

Grasslands and moorlands offer relatively little cover to birds, and some are harsh places where both water and food may be scarce. A number of birds found in these areas are ground-dwellers, and they are often well camouflaged, which makes them hard to spot unless flushed from their hiding places.

Moors and grasslands are among the best habitats in which to spot predatory birds as they fly overhead seeking live quarry or carcasses to scavenge. Prey species are also present in numbers, but they are more difficult to spot because of their camouflage.

Spotting predatory birds

Large predators and scavengers such as condors (Cathartidae) fly high over grasslands, utilizing the warm air

Left: The crested caracara (Caracara plancus), *native to the USA and South America, may survive by scavenging rather than hunting.*

Above: A male greater prairie chicken (Tympanuchus cupido) *shows off the barred plumage that is a feature of many birds found in moors and grasslands.*

currents known as thermals, which allow them to remain airborne with minimal effort. Smaller hunters such as hawks swoop down much lower over the open countryside as they search for the small mammals or birds that form the basis of their diet.

Grassland birds

Perhaps not surprisingly, many of the birds living in this type of habitat are primarily terrestrial, essentially because —with the exceptions of boulders, crags or low-lying shrubs—there is little room for them to perch. The plumage on their backs is frequently barred and mottled. This serves to break up their outline from above, making it harder for predators passing overhead to spot them. If disturbed at ground level, some grassland birds will take off almost vertically, often with a loud whirring of the wings, and then subsequently glide for a distance at a low level, before dropping back down

to the safety and cover of the vegetation. If pursued, they will take off again immediately, only staying on the ground once they feel secure.

Moorland camouflage

On moorlands and steppes the weather can become cold and snowy in winter. Some of the birds found in this terrain undergo a seasonal molt at the onset of winter, from which they emerge transformed by lighter-colored plumage to help conceal their presence.

Birdwatching tips

• Seek a good vantage point to increase your chances of spotting and following birds of prey.
• You will need a pair of powerful binoculars in grassland environments, as you will be combing relatively large and distant expanses of sky and land in search of birds.
• Use whatever natural cover is available to conceal your presence, such as tall vegetation and outcropping rocks.
• Horse riding can be a good way to cover long distances in grasslands and yet have a reasonable chance of spotting bird life, because birds are often less fearful of people on horseback.

Typical sightings in grassland habitats, depending to some extent on location:
• Eagles
• Vultures
• Grouse
• Hawks

Right: Avoiding predators is difficult in open countryside—especially hunters flying overhead. For prey species, the best strategy is to blend into the background and avoid being seen. While a relatively large number of mainly terrestrial birds are found in grasslands, therefore, these birds are often almost impossible to spot unless they take fright and fly up as you walk across the landscape. On the other hand, grasslands offer one of the best environments for observing birds of prey, since these birds are forced to spend relatively long periods on the wing searching for food.

1 Rough-legged hawk
2 Lark sparrows
3 Sage grouse
4 Burrowing owl
5 Prairie falcon
6 Western meadowlark
7 Lark bunting

URBAN LIFE

Some birds display a remarkable ability to adapt to modern life, occurring right in the center of cities.
They use buildings for nesting and, in the case of birds of prey, as vantage points for hunting, just as they
would use trees or rocky crags in the wild. City parks, in particular, have become major refuges for birds.

Cities, as densely populated areas, tend to be slightly warmer than the country-side, and this warm microclimate offers a number of advantages for birds. Drinking water is less likely to freeze in cold weather, and in spring, as plants bud and grow more quickly because of the warmth, insects are more readily available as food.

Residents and visitors

Some birds live permanently in cities, taking advantage of parks, whereas

Above: Many gulls have left their seaside haunts and moved inland, where they scavenge on leftovers and city dumps, often ripping apart plastic refuse sacks in search of food.

Above: Out of all birds, the feral pigeon (Columba livia) has adapted best to urban life, to the extent that it is now a common sight in cities around the world.

Below: Some birds of prey, such as this turkey vulture (Cathartes aura), have adapted to feed in cities. They will often feed on the carcasses of birds and other creatures killed by passing traffic, and are a common sight near refuse dumps, seeking anything edible there.

others are more casual visitors, flying in to roost at night from outlying areas, or pausing there on migration. Deserted buildings offer a snug and relatively safe retreat for birds that roost in flocks, whereas birds of prey seek the inaccessible ledges of high-rise buildings. The abundance of feral pigeons (*Columba livia*) in built-up areas attracts peregrine falcons (*Falco peregrinus*), proving that they are just as adaptable as their prey. The falcons may keep pigeon populations in check, but if not, their numbers can be also curbed by feeding them with corn, which acts as a contraceptive.

A life above the bustle of city streets generally offers predatory species a fairly safe existence, compared with more rural areas where they risk being shot illegally. There are still dangers lurking on the city streets, however. High-rise office blocks with large expanses of glass can lure birds to a fatal collision.

Migrating birds still pass through cities on occasion, notably huge flocks of common starlings (*Sturnus vulgaris*). These congregate not just in city parks, but also roost on buildings and tree-lined streets when breaking their journey, creating a noisy chatter and plenty of mess.

Birdwatching tips
• City parks offer the best chances of spotting the largest number of species in urban environments, particularly if there is a sizeable pond or lake.
• Early morning is a good time to spot birds at close quarters in cities, before many people are on the streets.
• Don't forget about the dangers of traffic in your enthusiasm to spot particular birds.
• Join the local ornithological society to gain insight into the more unusual species found in local towns and cities.

Typical sightings in urban environments, depending to some extent on location:
• Falcons
• Owls
• Pigeons and doves
• Gulls

Right: The spread of cities inevitably influences the local avian populations, by altering the neighboring habitat. When new development encroaches on surrounding land, for example, it becomes increasingly hard for birds that have fairly specialist feeding requirements, such as white storks, to obtain enough food for themselves and their young. Only opportunists such as pigeons are likely to thrive in crowded city centers, but a wider variety of birds use the oases of city parks.

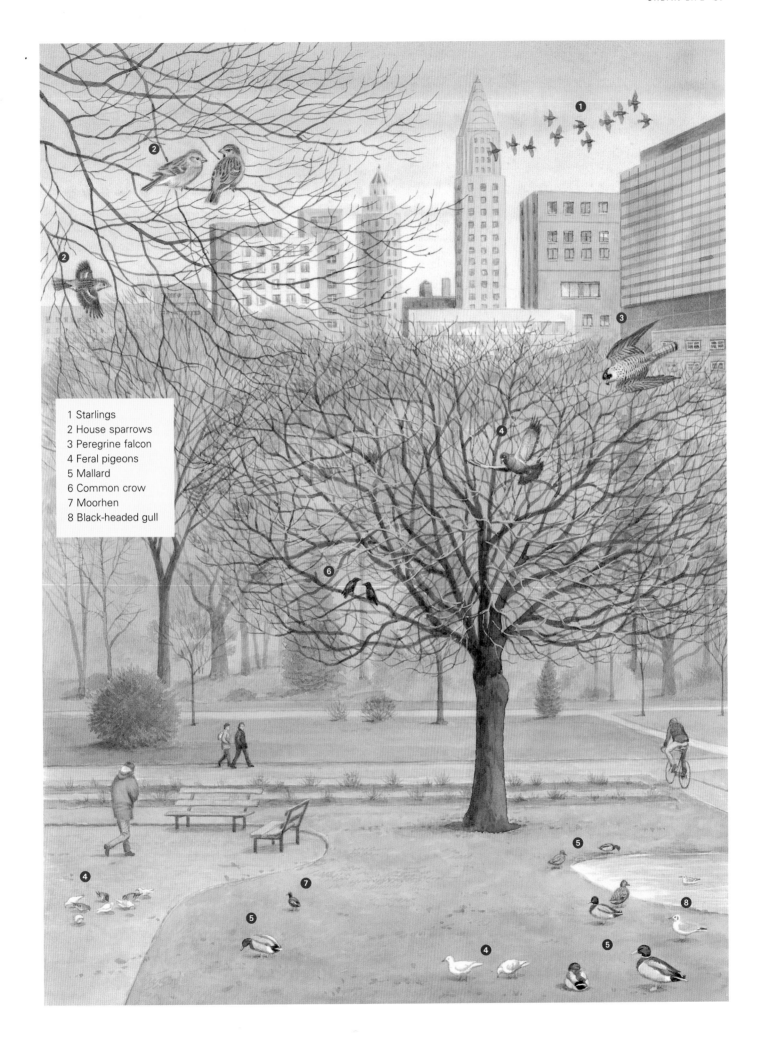

1 Starlings
2 House sparrows
3 Peregrine falcon
4 Feral pigeons
5 Mallard
6 Common crow
7 Moorhen
8 Black-headed gull

BACKYARDS

An amazing variety of birds have been recorded as backyard visitors. Cardinals, chickadees, sparrows and finches regularly visit bird tables, while jays, doves, woodpeckers and hummingbirds feed on the ground or from shrubs. Feeding stations help to attract birds, but they also visit as part of their natural behavior.

Tidy, immaculately manicured backyards generally support less bird life than well-established ones with plenty of mature shrubs that can be used for roosting and nesting. If there are stands of trees nearby, or lining the street outside, the range of birds visiting the backyard will increase, and larger species will become more common. Artificial nesting sites, such as nest boxes of various types and sizes, can also help to increase the variety and numbers of birds that visit backyards regularly.

Birds face a major backyard hazard in the guise of the domestic cat. Huge numbers of individuals fall victim to these pets annually. The majority of the casualties are young fledglings, which lack the awareness and caution of adult birds. In areas where the cat population is especially high, there

Above: Bird tables and feeders help to attract birds into gardens by providing them with additional food sources. These are especially valuable during cold winter weather.

may be local declines in bird numbers. However, studies suggest that bird populations do not seem to be adversely affected by cats overall.

Helpers and pests

Birds are often regarded as gardeners' friends because they help to control the number of invertebrate pests. For example, titmice (Paridae) eat aphids on rose bushes, and thrushes (*Turdus*) hunt snails. At certain times of year, however, some birds can themselves become pests. Pigeons (*Columba*) often dig up newly planted seeds and eat them before they can germinate, unless the seeds are protected in some way. Later in the year, some species eat ripening berries.

Residents and migrants

Some birds are resident in backyard settings throughout the year. Others are temporary visitors, migrating to warmer climates for the winter period. Hummingbirds (Trochilidae), for example, are resident in northern parts of North America for only part of the year, and head south for the winter. Meanwhile, winter migrants from further north may descend on these

backyard habitats in place of the species that have already left. Studies provide clear evidence that actual shifts in the behavior and distribution of birds are currently occurring because of the availability of the kind of habitat and the provision of food there. The Eurasian blackbird (*Turdus merula*) has now become a common sight in backyards, while, in North America, the American robin (*Turdus migratorius*) has moved from its traditional woodland haunts into this type of environment too.

Above: A wide choice of bird food is currently available, along with various types of feeder to dispense it. These American goldfinches (Carduelis tristis) have been photographed eating sunflower seeds.

Right: In many respects, backyards offer an ideal habitat for birds. Food is readily available in these surroundings, as well as trees and shrubs, which provide good opportunities for roosting and nesting. Unfortunately, backyards can often be dangerous places for birds to visit, thanks to the popularity of cats as pets. Nor are cats the only danger in this type of habitat. Predatory birds, notably magpies (Pica hudsonia), will raid the nests of smaller birds, taking both eggs and chicks.

Birdwatching tips

• You can encourage invertebrate-eating birds to visit your backyard by creating a wild area or by establishing a compost heap where invertebrates can multiply.

• Positioning a bird table near a window will allow you to watch birds from inside the house, but take care to site it well away from cover where cats could lurk and ambush the birds.

• Keep a pair of binoculars handy indoors so you can get a better view of the bird table and any unexpected visitors to it, plus a notepad to record descriptions of any unusual birds you see.

• Try to avoid using insecticides in your backyard, as these reduce the food that will be available for birds.

• Ordinary slug pellets will poison slug-eaters such as thrushes. Use pellets that are described as safe for birds instead.

Typical sightings in gardens, depending to some extent on location:
• Finches
• Tanagers
• Woodpeckers
• Hummingbirds

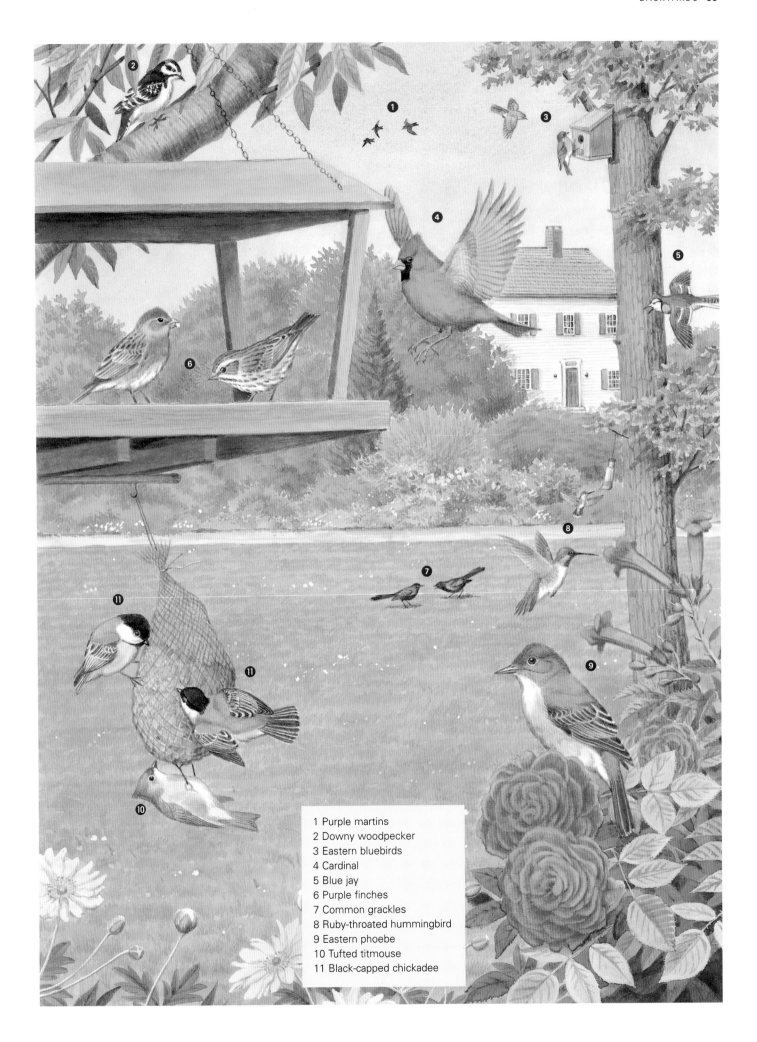

1 Purple martins
2 Downy woodpecker
3 Eastern bluebirds
4 Cardinal
5 Blue jay
6 Purple finches
7 Common grackles
8 Ruby-throated hummingbird
9 Eastern phoebe
10 Tufted titmouse
11 Black-capped chickadee

ENDANGERED SPECIES AND CONSERVATION

It has been estimated that three-quarters of the world's birds may come under threat in the 21st century. Habitat destruction poses the most serious danger, so conservationists are striving to preserve bird habitats worldwide. Direct intervention of various kinds is also used to ensure the survival of particular species.

Around the world, threats to birds are varied and complex, but most are linked to human interference in the ecosystem, and will thus continue to grow as human populations increase.

Habitat destruction

Habitat destruction includes the deforestation of the world's tropical rainforests, which host a wide variety of birds, and also the conversion of many grassland areas into crop fields or livestock pasture. The first casualties of habitat destruction are often species with specialized feeding or nesting requirements, which cannot easily adapt to change.

In recent years, there have been a number of instances of opportunistic species adapting and thriving in altered habitats. One example is the common mynah (*Acridotheres tristis*), whose natural distribution is centered on India but has been introduced to other locations worldwide, often to control locust numbers. Such success stories are the exception rather than the rule,

Below: Lear's macaw (Anodorhynchus leari)— native to Bahia, Brazil—is one of the most endangered of all South American parrots, with probably fewer than 150 left in the wild.

Above: The northern spotted owl (Strix occidentalis caurina) is currently threatened by the rapid felling of the ancient forests on the west coast of California.

however. Generally, the diversity of bird life in an area declines drastically when the land is modified or cleared.

Hunting and pollution

Unregulated hunting of adult birds, eggs or young threatens a variety of species worldwide. The birds may be killed for their meat or feathers, or captured live and sold through the pet trade. In many countries, laws are now in place to protect rare species, but hunting and trading still go on illegally.

Overfishing is a related hazard facing seabirds, especially now that trawling methods have become so efficient. Global shortages of fish stocks are forcing fishermen to target fish that had previously been of little commercial value, but that are an important part of seabirds' diets.

In agricultural areas, pesticides and herbicides sprayed on farmers' fields decimate bird populations by eliminating their plant or animal food supplies. The deliberate or accidental release of industrial chemicals into the air, water or soil is another hazard, while in the oceans, seabirds are killed by dumped toxins and oil spills. Disease is another major threat that may increase.

Climate change

In the near future, global warming caused by increased emissions of carbon dioxide and other gases is likely to impact on many bird habitats, and will almost certainly adversely affect birds' food supplies. If plants or other foods become unavailable in an area, birds must adapt their feeding habits or face extinction. As temperatures rise, the melting of the polar ice caps will threaten seabird populations by destroying their traditional nesting areas. Rising sea levels will also threaten low-lying wetlands favored by wading birds.

Threats to island birds

Some of the world's most distinctive birds have evolved in relative isolation on islands. Unfortunately, these species are also extremely vulnerable to changes in their environment, partly because their populations are small. One of the greatest threats comes from

Above: This guillemot (Uria aalge) *killed in Scottish waters is just one of the countless avian victims claimed by oil spillages each year. Large spills of oil can have devastating effects on whole populations.*

introduced predators, particularly domestic cats. Cats have been responsible for wiping out a host of island species, including the flightless Stephen Island wren (*Xenicus lyalli*) of New Zealand waters, which became extinct in 1894, thanks to the lighthouse-keeper's cat.

Cats are not the only introduced predators that can cause serious harm to avian populations. Grazing animals such as goats, introduced to islands by passing ships to provide future crews with fresh meat, have frequently destroyed the native vegetation, so reducing the birds' food supply.

Today, control of harmful introduced species is helping to save surviving populations of endangered birds on islands such as the Galapagos off Ecuador, home to the flightless cormorant (*Phalacrocorax harrisi*) and other rare birds.

Conservation and captive-breeding

Preserving habitat is the best and most cost-effective way to ensure the survival of all the birds that frequent a particular ecosystem. A worldwide network of national parks and reserves now helps to protect at least part of many birds' habitats. In addition,

conservationists may take a variety of direct measures to safeguard the future of particular species, such as launching a captive-breeding program. This approach has proven effective in increasing numbers of various critically endangered species, from the Californian condor (*Gymnogyps californianus*) of the USA, to the echo parakeet (*Psittacula echo*) of Mauritius. In some cases, the technique of artificial insemination has been used to fertilize the eggs.

Artificially or naturally fertilized eggs can be transferred to incubators to be hatched, effectively doubling the number of chicks that can be reared. This is because removing the eggs often stimulates the hen to lay again more quickly than usual. Hand-rearing chicks on formulated diets helps to ensure the survival of the young once hatched. When hand-reared chicks are later released into the wild, it is vital that they bond with their own species and retain their natural fear of people, so glove puppets shaped like the parent birds are often used to feed the chicks.

Reintroduction programs

Breeding endangered species is relatively easy compared with the difficulties of reintroducing a species to an area of its former habitat. The cost of such reintroduction programs is

Above: Glove puppets resembling the parent bird's head are often used when hand-rearing chicks, such as this peregrine falcon (Falco peregrinus), *to encourage the birds to bond with their own kind when eventually released.*

often very high. Staff are needed not only to look after the aviary stock and rear the chicks, but also to carry out habitat studies. These assess the dangers that the birds will face after release and pinpoint release sites. The newly released birds must then be monitored, which may include fitting them with radio transmitters.

Ecotourism

Working with local people and winning their support is often essential to the long-term success of conservation programs. This approach has been used successfully on some of the Caribbean islands, such as St Vincent, home to various indigenous Amazon parrots (*Amazona*). Increasing clearance of the islands' forests, a growing human population and hunting all threatened these birds.

Effective publicity about these rare parrots, including portrayals of them on currency and postage stamps, helped to raise local people's awareness of the birds as part of their islands' heritage. A publicity campaign brought the parrots' plight to international attention and attracted visitors to the region, which brought in much-needed foreign currency. Thus, so-called "ecotourism" both helped the local economy and enlisted the islanders' support to conserve the parrots.

Left: The rapid destruction of the world's rainforests, seen here in Costa Rica, is the single most important threat facing tropical birds.

CLASSIFICATION

The way in which different birds are grouped is known as classification. This is not only helpful in terms of distinguishing individual species and those that are closely related, but it also enables wider assessments of relationships between larger groups to be made.

Interest in how best to group birds into distinct categories is nothing new. It dates back nearly 2,500 years to the ancient Greeks, when an early method of classification was developed by the philosopher Aristotle. He sought to group living creatures on the basis of differences in their lifestyles, rather than on the basis of anatomical distinctions, which are favored today. The first modern attempt to trace relationships between birds was made by Sir Francis Willoughby, in a book entitled *Ornithologia*, which was published in 1676. Willoughby saw the need for what was essentially an identification key that would enable readers to find an unknown bird by means of special tables devised for this purpose.

Willoughby's work concentrated solely on birds, but it was actually a Swedish botanist, Carl von Linné (also known as Linnaeus), who devised the universal system of classification that is now known as the Linnean System. Linné relied primarily on the physical similarities between living organisms as the basis for grouping them, laying the

Below: The nominate subspecies of the pearly conure (Pyrrhura lepida lepida) is identifiable by its distinctive red markings on the wing.

Above: One of the recognized subspecies of the pearly conure (Pyrrhura lepida anerythra), which differs subtley from its relative below.

foundations for the science of classification, which is now known as systematics. He refined this approach through a series of new editions of his classic work *Systema Naturae*, which was originally published in 1735 for the first time.

Linné's system operates through a series of ranks, creating what is sometimes described as a hierarchic method. Starting from a very general base, the ranks become increasingly specific, splitting into smaller groups, until, finally, individual types of birds can be identified. One advantage of this system is that when a new species is discovered, it can be fitted easily into this existing framework.

New advances

While Linnaeus and successive generations of taxonomists relied on physical similarities, the use of D.N.A. analysis is currently transforming our understanding of the natural world. By comparing sequences of the genetic material D.N.A., it is possible for ornithologists to investigate which birds share D.N.A. sequences that suggest a close relationship. This method of study is set to revolutionize taxonomy and is already leading to numerous revisions of the existing classification of birds.

How the system works

Birds, as animals, belong to the Kingdom Animalia, and, since they have backbones, are members of the phylum Chordata, which includes all vertebrates. The class Aves is the first division at which birds are separated

Above: The green plumage of the African race of ringnecked parakeet (Psittacula krameri krameri) *tends to be of a more yellowish shade, and the bill is dark.*

from other vertebrates such as mammals. Birds alone comprise this major grouping, which is subdivided into smaller categories called orders. It is then a matter of tracking an individual species down through the various ranks of classification. For example, the classificatory breakdown of the pearly conure is as follows:
Order: Psittaciformes
Family: Psittacidae
Genus: *Pyrrhura*
Species: *Pyrrhura lepida*
Subspecies: *Pyrrhura lepida lepida; Pyrrhura lepida anerythra; Pyrrhura lepida coerulescens*
If you are unsure where you are in the ranking, the way in which the names are written gives a clear indication. The names of orders end in "-formes," while family names terminate with "-idae." At or below genus level, all names are italicized, with the genus comprising one or more species. The scientific name of a species always consists of two descriptions, with the genus names being written first.

Species are the basic fundamental level in the taxonomic tree, enabling particular types of birds to be named individually. Members of a particular species generally identify with each other and do not normally interbreed with other species. However, if interbreeding does occur, the resulting offspring are known as hybrids.

At the most specific level of the taxonomic tree are subspecies: closely related forms of the same species that are nevertheless distinct enough to be identified separately. These are often defined on the basis of their size, and also because of marked differences in coloration. In the case of the pearly conure (*Pyrrhura lepida lepida*), the nominate form (meaning the first form to be recognized) can be distinguished by the repetition of the "trivial" name, *lepida*. Other races of this South American parrot boast a similar appearance to the nominate subspecies, but often with subtle differences in color on the head and wings.

It was Linné himself who devised this method of distinguishing between such closely related individuals, first describing it in 1758. His method is sometimes known as the trinomial

system, reflecting the fact that the name of the subspecies is made up of three parts.

What's in a name?
Even the choice of scientific names is not random. They give an insight into a bird's appearance or distribution, using descriptions derived from Latin. The name *flavinucha*, for example, indicates yellow plumage around the neck; the description *peruviana* in the case of the parrot-billed seed eater (*Sporophila peruviana*) indicates that the bird's habitat is in South America. In a few instances, the species' description features a person's name, for example *Calypte Anna*, popularly known as Anna's hummingbird. It was so-called in 1829 by the noted French naturalist Rene Lesson, to honor the beauty of an Italian noblewoman of the period—Anna, Duchess of Rivoli.

In order to be formally recognized as a species, an example of the bird concerned, known as the "type specimen," has to be held in a museum collection, where a detailed description of its characteristics is written up as part of the identification process.

Below: Subtle differences in color can be seen in the Indian race of ringnecked parakeet (Psittacula krameri manillensis), *which is now established in some parts of the USA, most notably in the vicinity of Bakersfield, California.*

DIRECTORY OF BIRDS

Recognizing birds is not always easy, particularly if you have only a relatively brief sighting. This part of the book has therefore been designed to simplify the task of identification as much as possible, by allowing you to link your sightings with the environment in which you spotted the bird. The section is divided into the particular habitats where birds are most likely to be spotted. It should be pointed out that this system is not infallible, as some birds are highly adaptable and range widely through different environments, but it is a useful starting point. Distribution maps accompanying all the illustrated entries provide a visual guide as to exactly where bird species are to be found within these regions, while the text provides information on the time of year and locations where the birds are most likely to be seen, in the case of migratory species.

The associated descriptions will help to clarify whether you have seen a cock bird or a hen, since there are often plumage differences between the sexes. Other information in these fact boxes about habitat, feeding and breeding habits should provide further help when it comes to identifying a particular bird. A bird's general shape, and the characteristic way in which it moves and behaves, all add up to what birdwatchers call its "jizz," which can help to identify birds even from a tiny speck in the sky or a dark shape scuttling behind a hedge.

Not every species in America is covered, but the representative sample featured in the following pages means that you should at least be able to identify the type of bird you spotted. Browsing through these pages also affords an opportunity to learn more about the varying lifestyles of America's birds, ranging from parrots living in the lush Amazon rainforests to the bitterly cold breeding grounds of puffins on the Alaskan peninsula, and the various pigeons and predatory birds that inhabit our city centers.

Note: Where an (E) appears after the scientific name of a bird, this indicates that it is an endangered species.

Left: Flamingos (Phoenicopteridae), one of the avian families present in America, often inhabit quite harsh environnments.

BIRDS OF AMERICA

There is a significant divide between the avifauna of the South American continent, and those families represented in North America, with the Central American isthmus serving as a crossover zone. This is partly a reflection of the feeding habits of the birds, with many fruit-eating species of the Amazonian region, for example, being restricted to this rainforest area, where they are guaranteed a constant supply of food throughout the year. Some of the most unusual birds in the world, including toucans with their bizarre and often colorful bills, are found in this region and nowhere else. Hummingbirds, which include the smallest bird in the world, do range across both continents, and through the Caribbean, although they reach their greatest diversity on the southern continent. The localized distribution of some birds in parts of South America, combined with the often inaccessible terrain, means that new species are still found there quite regularly.

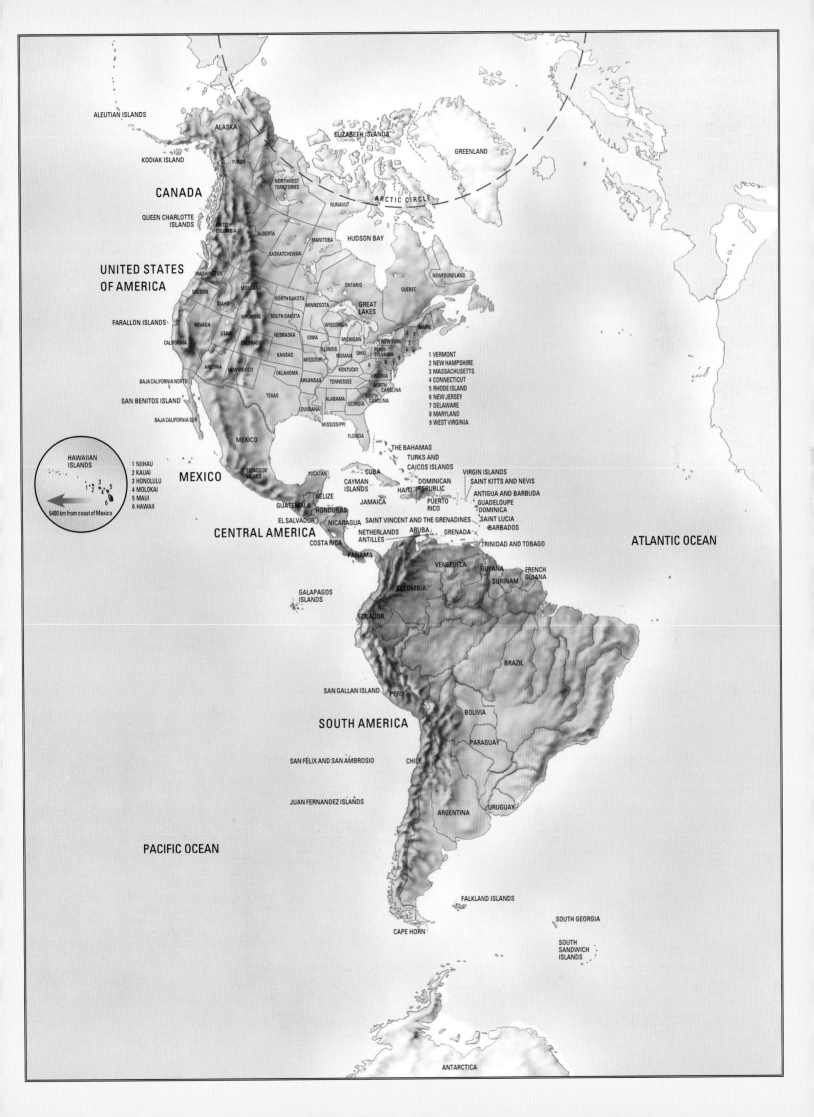

OCEAN WANDERERS

These birds often have a wide distribution, roaming far out from the shore over the oceans.
They may return to land only in order to nest, often choosing remote islands for this purpose,
so they are not likely to be seen by the casual observer. However, they may be attracted
to passing ships in search of offerings of food.

Long-tailed jaeger

Stercorarius longicaudus

The long tail feathers of this jaeger account for as much as 9in (23cm) of its overall length, and it is actually still the smallest member of this group of seabirds. Long-tailed jaegers breed in the Arctic region of North America, spending the winter at sea. Only on rare occasions are they observed on freshwater lakes.

Jaegers can be considered the pirates of the skies, menacing gulls and terns and harrying them to drop fish or other quarry, which they quickly swoop down on and seize before the prey falls into the water. The long-tailed jaeger is especially agile in flight, as reflected by its long, pointed wings, while its hooked bill is a formidable weapon. On occasion, long-tailed jaegers may resort to attacking other nesting seabirds, taking both their eggs and the chicks.

Identification:
Characteristic long, narrow tail feathers. Underparts are whitish, with a grayer tone on the flanks and around the vent. Head is blackish and the wings are dark. Sexes are alike.

Distribution: Occurring throughout the far north of North America and Greenland during the breeding period in the summer. Then flies south to spend the winter around the coast of South America and the western side of South Africa extending down into sub-Antarctic areas.
Size: 23in (58cm).
Habitat: Mainly open sea.
Nest: Depression on the ground.
Eggs: 1–2, olive with dark spots.
Food: Fish and other animal matter.

Fork-tailed storm petrel

Gray storm petrel *Oceanodroma furcata*

The bluish coloration of the fork-tailed petrel sets it apart from all other related species. These birds are most likely to be seen over open sea, swooping down to break the surface of the water occasionally with their legs. They feed both on the wing and on the sea surface. Like other storm petrels, they come ashore to breed, often on islands, seeking the security of underground burrows at this time. Breeding colonies can be savaged by introduced mammals, notably cats and rats. The nostrils of fork-tailed petrels are located in a tube above the bill, and serve to excrete excess salt from the body, ingested as a result of the bird's environment and diet.

Identification: Distinctive bluish-gray plumage is lighter on the throat and the undertail coverts. The tail is forked, and the wings are a duskier shade of blue. Both the bill and the legs are black. The plumage around the eyes is mainly black. Sexes are alike.

Distribution: North American west coast south to California. Also present on the Aleutians and neighboring islands.
Size: 9in (23cm).
Habitat: Open sea.
Nest: Underground burrow.
Eggs: 1, white.
Food: Fish, invertebrates and plankton.

Black storm petrel (*Oceanodroma melania*): 9in (23cm)
Extends along the Californian coastline and offshore islands. This is the most common and largest of the black-colored petrels, with a pale wing bar and a relatively slow flight pattern. Calls at night from underground burrows. Sexes are alike.

Black-footed albatross (*Diomedea nigripes*): 36in (91cm)
Found in the northern Pacific Ocean extending from western North America to the Asiatic coast. Lives on the open seas. Predominantly brownish gray with a white face and undertail coverts, although occasionally paler. Feet are black. Sexes are alike.

Waved albatross (*Diomedea irrorata*): 37in (94cm)
Occurs off the northwest coast of South America, west to the Galapagos Islands. Easily recognized by the combination of a whitish head and neck with a yellow suffusion, plus brown plumage elsewhere on the body. May be observed feeding at night, when squid are nearer the surface. Sexes are alike.

White-tailed tropic bird (*Phaethon lepturus*): 32in (81cm)
Virtually pantropical distribution, but absent from the eastern Pacific. Smallest of the tropic birds. Slender shape, mainly white, occasionally a very pale rosy or peach color, with distinctive black bars in an almost V-shaped formation across the back. Another black area is evident toward the end of each wing. Young birds lack the long tail (which accounts for half the total length of the adult) and have extensive barring on their upperparts.

Laysan albatross

Diomedea immutabilis

The Laysan is the most common albatross of the northern Pacific region. According to reports of sightings, especially from the larger islands, these birds now appear to be venturing closer to the shoreline of the Hawaiian islands. Unlike many albatrosses, the Laysan rarely follows ships, and comes to land only during the breeding season. It is thought that pairs remain together for life, and albatrosses rank among the longest-lived of all birds, having a life expectancy often exceeding half a century. They face few natural enemies, but sadly more are dying prematurely after seizing baited hooks intended for fish left on long lines by fishing boats. Albatrosses usually scoop up prey from the ocean surface while in flight.

Distribution: Extends from the northern Pacific Ocean to the western coast of North America. Especially common on Midway and Laysan islands, Hawaii.
Size: 36in (91cm).
Habitat: Open sea.
Nest: Area of ground.
Eggs: 1, white, may be blotched.
Food: Fish and other aquatic creatures.

Identification: Relatively small. Predominantly white with a sooty-brown back, upper wings and tail and dark feathering around the eyes. In flight, the largish, pinkish feet extend beyond the tail. Yellow curved bill has a black tip. Sexes alike.

Hawaiian petrel

Dark-rumped petrel *Pterodroma phaeopygia* (E)

The alternative name of dark-rumped petrel is not a clear guide to identification, since various petrels display this feature. The Hawaiian petrel appears to be quite rare compared to other species and is thought to be declining in numbers. It spends its time at sea, coming onto land to breed. The largest colony is found around the Haleakala Crater on Maui. These petrels nest in underground burrows, remaining there during the day and emerging to search for food at night. Outside the breeding period, Hawaiian petrels are most likely to be sighted to the southeast of the Hawaiian islands.

Identification: Black upperparts, with white plumage just above the bill and extending right across the underparts. The underside of the wings are also mainly white, with a black area evident on each of the leading edges when seen from below. There is usually a white, V-shaped marking present at the base of the uppertail coverts, above the tail. Sexes are alike.

Distribution: Pacific Ocean, Hawaii and Galapagos Islands.
Size: 17in (43cm).
Habitat: Open sea.
Nest: Underground burrow.
Eggs: 1, white.
Food: Fish and other aquatic creatures.

SEABIRDS

Although they feed mainly on fish, these birds have evolved quite different feeding strategies, ranging from the pelican's sieve-like bill that acts like a trawl, to the targeted diving and underwater swimming of the cormorants. Another group, typified by the frigatebirds, relies on others to do the hard work of catching fish, and resorts to mugging them to seize their catches as they fly back to land.

Man o'war bird

Magnificent frigatebird *Fregata magnificens*

Distribution: Throughout the eastern Pacific Ocean, Gulf of Mexico and tropical parts of the Atlantic Ocean.
Size: 40in (101cm).
Habitat: Oceanic coastlines.
Nest: Platform of sticks.
Eggs: 1, white.
Food: Fish and invertebrates, including jellyfish. Also preys on baby turtles and seabird chicks.

These birds can glide for long periods, relying on their huge 7½ft (229cm) wingspan to help keep them airborne on the air currents. The male's throat patch, prominent at close quarters, is far less visible when in the air. Pairs nest on the coast in areas where there are other smaller, fish-eating seabirds that can be harried for their catches, so that the frigatebirds do not have to obtain their own food. If necessary, however, they often catch flying fish, as well as other creatures found near the surface, including baby turtles. It is believed that although cock birds may breed annually if the opportunity is there, most hens nest only every second year.

Identification: Jet black, with a bare, bright red throat patch that can be inflated for display purposes. Hens are similar, but can be easily distinguished by white feathering on the breast. In immature birds, the plumage on the head is also white.

American white pelican

Rough-billed pelican *Pelecanus erythrorhynchos*

These pelicans are found mainly on stretches of fresh water, sometimes hunting in groups for fish and other creatures such as crayfish. Occasionally, they may fly long distances to obtain food if the waters that they inhabit have a low fish population. On migration, American white pelicans fly over land rather than the ocean, although populations in the southern part of their range will remain in the same region throughout the year. These birds breed communally, usually on quite inaccessible islands. Their chicks associate together in groups, known as pods, before they are fully fledged.

Above: The pelican's pouch is used to trawl for food.

Identification: Predominantly white plumage with contrasting black primary flight feathers. The large yellow bill develops a distinctive raised area on the ridge toward the tip from late winter through the breeding season. Sexes are alike, but the female is smaller.

Distribution: Western and central areas of North America, extending as far south as Guatemala and Costa Rica during the winter.
Size: 70in (178cm).
Habitat: Both freshwater and saltwater areas, not ranging far out to sea.
Nest: On the ground.
Eggs: 2–3, whitish with darker markings.
Food: Fish and other aquatic creatures.

Double-crested cormorant

Phalacrocorax auritus

These cormorants are found mainly in coastal waters, sometimes using unorthodox sites such as wrecked ships as perches. They also venture to inland areas, where they are found on suitable stretches of water. They can form large flocks, often hunting together for fish, which form the bulk of their diet. In the past, double-crested cormorant numbers have plummeted in some parts of their range because of DDT entering the food chain. This pesticide has had a harmful effect on eggshell thickness, and, as a result, has significantly reduced the number of chicks that hatch. The ban on DDT has seen their numbers rise again. These cormorants have also benefited from the increasing number of freshwater reservoirs in various parts of their range, providing them with additional areas of habitat.

Identification: Adults are entirely black. Immature birds show a whitish hue to their underparts. A double crest of feathers is evident on the back of the head during the breeding period, with a variable amount of white coloration. Has bare yellowish-orange skin around the face, with a powerful hooked bill. Females are smaller in size. Several different races are recognized through their range, differing in the extent of the white feathering forming the crest, as well as in the depth of coloration.

Distribution: Much of the USA, south to parts of Central America in the winter. Also in parts of the Caribbean, from Florida to Cuba.
Size: 36in (91cm).
Habitat: Areas of freshwater and seawater.
Nest: Built of sticks and often seaweed.
Eggs: 3–4, pale blue.
Food: Fish and other aquatic creatures.

Brown pelican (*Pelecanus occidentalis*): 54in (137cm)
Coastal areas from southern USA south into South America. Dark brown in color, with an area of white feathering on the head and neck. The bill is normally held flat against the neck on land, and used for trawling for fish in the water. Hens slightly smaller in size.

Blue-eyed cormorant (Imperial shag, *Phalacrocorax atriceps*): 30in (76cm)
Southern South America, from Chile to Argentina and Uruguay, and the Falkland Islands. Loose black crest with black plumage extending from above the upper bill over the head, back and wings to the tail. White on the sides of the head down over the underparts, with white patches on the wings. Blue skin encircling the eyes. Sexes alike.

Rock cormorant (Magellan shag, *Phalacrocorax magellanicus*): 28in (71cm)
Extends from the Pacific around to the Atlantic coast of South America; also present on the Falkland Islands. Distinctive patch of white feathering on the cheeks, with reddish skin encircling the eyes. Otherwise mainly black, with white chest and underparts. Sexes alike.

Pink-footed shearwater (*Puffinus creatopus*): 19in (48cm)
Occurs in the eastern Pacific, extending off the coast of the Americas. Also on Hawaii. Grayish-brown, and paler underparts with a variable amount of mottled brown coloration. Flesh-pink bill with dark tip. Sexes and young birds alike.

Rhinoceros auklet

Cerorhinca monocerata

These auklets congregate in areas where they can come ashore and excavate their nests in relative safety. They breed communally, with nesting densities of approximately 7 birds per square yard (square meter) having been recorded on Forrester Island, Alaska. Rhinoceros auklets dig long underground tunnels, using their bills and feet to excavate these burrows during the night. It will typically take a pair about 14 nights to construct an average tunnel about 7ft (213cm) long. The hen lays a single egg in a chamber at the end.

Identification: Sooty-black upperparts. Underparts from the chin down to the chest and flanks are whitish, with a brownish-gray tone especially evident on the breast. White streaks on the face, creating a mustached effect, plus white crests extending from the eyes back to the nape of the neck that are less distinctive outside the breeding season. Orangish bill with characteristic horn-like swelling at the base of the upper bill, which largely disappears during the winter. Sexes are alike.

Distribution: Western coast of North America, extending to the Aleutian Islands across the Bering Sea.
Size: 15in (38cm).
Habitat: Coastal areas.
Nest: Underground chamber, may be lined with vegetation.
Eggs: 1, white spotted.
Food: Fish, such as anchovies, sand launce and herrings.

PENGUINS, BOOBIES AND SEA DUCKS

Bright plumage is not generally a feature associated with seabirds, where more subdued hues of black, brown or white predominate. There are exceptions, however, most notably in the case of some ducks that have spread to the marine environment from the freshwater haunts more usually occupied by these waterfowl. These birds are also more predatory by nature.

Galapagos penguin

Sphensiscus mendiculus

These penguins have colonized the volcanic outcrops of the Galapagos Islands, seeking out fish such as sardines that feature prominently in their diet in coastal waters. Galapagos penguins usually fish together in pairs but hunt in larger groups sometimes too. When there is a change in the pattern of the ocean currents, owing to El Niño, and fish then become scarce, penguin numbers may plummet. This decline occurred most dramatically in the early 1980s, when just a few hundred Galapagos penguins survived. Their numbers have since undergone a good recovery, aided by the fact that they can breed throughout the year.

Above: Penguins may not be able to fly, but their wings make powerful flippers underwater.

Distribution: Confined to the Galapagos Islands.
Size: 21in (53cm).
Habitat: Coastal regions.
Nest: In caves or crevices.
Eggs: 2, whitish.
Food: Fish.

Identification: A relatively small penguin, especially when compared with related species. A very thin white stripe extends from the eye around the throat, and the sides of the face are dark. White area under the lower bill and over much of the underparts, apart from an uneven, mainly black circle of feathers. Bill is pinkish at the base. Sexes are alike, and patterning is less clearly defined in young birds.

Blue-faced booby

Masked booby *Sula dactylatra*

The blue-faced is the largest of the boobies, and preys upon correspondingly larger fish, swallowing those of up to 16in (41cm) without difficulty. Although these birds often dive quite deeply in search of fish, they may also catch flying fish at the surface. They sometimes lose their catch to frigatebirds that harry them as they fly back to land. Blue-faced boobies live in colonies, and prefer to nest on cliff faces. On remote islands in the absence of major predators, however, pairs may breed on the ground. While the hen is likely to lay two eggs, only one chick is normally reared, and the weaker chick loses out to its stronger sibling in the competition for food. Blue-faced boobies are long lived, and young birds may not breed until their third year. Sadly, the number of these birds is declining in some areas because increased development is disturbing their habitat. A large population can be found around the Galapagos Islands, off the western coast of South America.

Distribution: Pan-global around the equator. Occurs both on the Pacific and Atlantic sides of America, and in the Caribbean.
Size: 36in (91cm).
Habitat: Tropical oceans.
Nest: Accumulated droppings.
Eggs: 2, pale blue.
Food: Mainly fish.

Identification: Predominantly white but with black on the wings and a distinctive black tail. Has dark feathering on the face around the eyes, with a bluish tinge extending onto the yellowish bill. In hens the bill is significantly duller.

Gentoo penguin (*Pygoscelis papua*):
32in (81cm)
Northerly distribution extends to Uruguay on the Atlantic coast of South America, ranging south to the Antarctic Peninsula. No lines on the face, and the upperparts are blackish apart from a distinctive white area above each eye. Underparts are white. Bill is mainly pinkish. Sexes are alike.

Humbolt penguin (*Spheniscus humboldti*):
28in (71cm)
Occurs in the vicinity of the Humbolt Current along the shores of Chile and Peru. Distinctive pink fleshy edges at the base of the bill. Otherwise black and white, with a prominent white area on the throat. Sexes are alike.

Surf scoter (*Melanitta perspicillata*):
22in (56cm)
Coastal waters of North America, extending on the western seaboard south from western Alaska. Breeds in freshwater and overwinters at sea. White patch on forehead and on the nape; rest of the plumage is blackish, with a brightly colored bill. Hen is brown overall, with whitish areas on the sides of the face, and more blackish on the top of the head. Bill is grayish.

Peruvian booby (*Sula variegata*): 30in (76cm)
Usually ranges down from south Peru to Chile; sometimes found as far north as southern Colombia. White plumage on the head down across the underparts. Wings and back are brown with white mottling. Brown tail and flight feathers. Bill is purplish gray. Sexes are alike.

King eider

Somateria spectabilis

Like most birds from the far north, the king eider has a circumpolar distribution that reaches right around the top of the globe. Seasonal movements of these sea ducks tend to be more widespread than in other eiders, and they are remarkably common, with the North American population being estimated at as many as two million individuals. Huge groups of up to 100,000 birds will congregate together during the molting period, although the groups split up during the breeding season when pairs nest individually across the Arctic tundra. King eiders are powerful swimmers and generally dive to obtain their food.

Identification: Orange area edged with black above the reddish bill in breeding condition. Light-gray plumage extends down the neck. Chest is pale pinkish white, with black wings and underparts. Ducks are mainly a speckled shade of brown, and the pale underside of their wings is visible in flight. In eclipse plumage, drakes are a darker shade of brown, with an orangish-yellow bill and white plumage on the back.

Distribution: Largely within the Arctic Circle.
Size: 25½in (63cm).
Habitat: Tundra and open sea.
Nest: Hollow lined with down feathers.
Eggs: 4–7, olive buff.
Food: Predominantly crustaceans and marine invertebrates.

Oldsquaw

Long-tailed duck *Clangula hyemalis*

These sea ducks often congregate in large numbers, although in winter females and young birds tend to migrate further south in flocks than do adult drakes. They spend most of their time on the water, and obtain food by diving under the waves. They come ashore onto the tundra to nest, and ducks lay their eggs on the ground. The drakes soon return to the ocean, where they start to molt. When migrating, they generally fly quite low in lines, rather than in any other organized formation.

Identification: Black head, neck and chest, with white around the eyes and white underparts. Head becomes white across the top outside the breeding season, with patches of black evident on the sides. Gray rather than brown predominates on the wings. Long tail plumes present throughout the year. The smaller ducks undergo a similar transformation, and the sides of the face become white rather than blackish.

Distribution: Northern coasts, with circumpolar range. Winters farther south.
Size: 19in (47cm).
Habitat: Coastal waters and bays.
Nest: Hidden in vegetation or under a rock.
Eggs: 5–7, olive buff.
Food: Mainly crustaceans and marine invertebrates.

FLAMINGOS AND OTHER LARGER WATERBIRDS

A number of relatively large birds, ranging from flamingos to cranes and storks, have evolved to live in wetland areas, where their height can be an advantage in detecting food and wading through the water. Unfortunately, some have become so specialized in their habits that changes in their environment can have serious consequences for them, as in the case of flamingos.

American flamingo

Phoenicopterus ruber

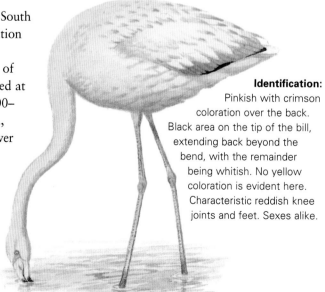

The distinctive coloration of these birds comes from their diet of algae or small creatures that have eaten the microscopic plants. They feed in a unique fashion by walking along with their heads submerged, their long necks allowing them to filter relatively large quantities of water by sweeping their unusually shaped bills from side to side. As a result of their highly specific feeding requirements, American flamingos are vulnerable to habitat loss or pollution of the shallow coastal lagoons that they inhabit. Young are reared on nests of mud raised above the water level, and are covered in a whitish-gray down at first. At a month old, they molt into a brownish down. Their bills are short and straight at this stage. American flamingos are known to live for more than 30 years in the wild.

Identification: Bright, almost reddish plumage on the neck, with a paler pink body. Bill also has a pink hue behind the black tip. Outstretched wings in flight show black areas. Sexes are alike.

Distribution: Caribbean islands, Mexico, the north coast of South America and the Galapagos Islands. Other races found in parts of southern Europe, Africa and Madagascar, extending through the Red Sea into Asia.
Size: 57in (145cm) tall.
Habitat: Shallow saline lagoons.
Nest: Mud.
Eggs: 1, white.
Food: Small mollusks, crustaceans and plant matter.

Chilean flamingo

Phoenicopterus chilensis

Distribution: Ranges from highlands of Peru to Tierra del Fuego, at the tip of the continent.
Size: Up to 41in (105cm) tall. Hens shorter and smaller.
Habitat: Highland salt lakes.
Nest: Mud.
Eggs: 1, white.
Food: Algae and invertebrates.

This is the most widely distributed South American flamingo, with a population extending more than 2,500 miles (4,000km). In the altiplano region of the Andes, they are usually observed at altitudes of 11,500– 15,000ft (3,500– 4,500m), but in parts of Argentina, east of the Andes, they occur at lower levels. In suitable areas, Chilean flamingos will congregate in large numbers, and as many as 100,000 have been counted on Lake Poopo in Bolivia. Lake Titicaca, found on the Bolivian border with Peru, is home to even greater numbers. Their calls are similar to the honking notes of geese.

Identification: Pinkish with crimson coloration over the back. Black area on the tip of the bill, extending back beyond the bend, with the remainder being whitish. No yellow coloration is evident here. Characteristic reddish knee joints and feet. Sexes alike.

Wood stork

Wood ibis *Mycteria americana*

Although usually it is most likely to be encountered in freshwater areas, the wood stork may be seen in mangrove swamps where food is abundant. These birds are opportunistic predators, and are equipped with a powerful bill to seize creatures ranging from fish to young turtles and alligators. These large birds breed colonially, often on nesting sites surrounded by water. Up to 50 pairs or more may be found in the same area where conditions are favorable. Pairs accomplish nest-building quite quickly, in about three days, and the hen lays the eggs on a nest lining of leaves. These storks are long lived, and their young are therefore slow to mature, often not breeding until they are five years old.

Identification: Bare, dark and unfeathered head is offset against the white plumage. The black feathering is confined to the wings and tail. Long bill, powerful at its base. White plumage in young birds tends to appear slightly soiled.

Distribution: Southern parts of the USA south as far as northwest Argentina.
Size: 47in (119cm).
Habitat: Marshland and lakes.
Nest: Made of sticks.
Eggs: 2–5, creamy white.
Food: Fish, amphibians and crustaceans.

Andean flamingo (*Phoenicoparrus andinus*): 63in (160cm)
In spite of its name, this flamingo has a much more restricted distribution than the Chilean, being found only in Chile and northwest Argentina. Purplish-red plumage on the head and neck. Yellow legs. Sexes are alike.

American anhinga (snakebird, *Anhinga anhinga*): 36in (91cm)
From eastern coastal areas of the USA south through Central America, and east of the Andes as far south as northern Argentina. Black with silvery-gray markings on the wings and tail. Hens are brown on the head and neck, with no crest. The powerful bill is used to spear prey underwater, including snakes.

Black-necked stilt (black-winged stilt, *Himantopus himantopus*): 15in (38cm)
Widely distributed from the southern USA south through South America. Also present in the Caribbean, Galapagos Islands and Hawaii. Predominantly white body, black wings and bill, with black on the head and neck. Pinkish legs. Hens have brownish-black backs.

Hudsonian godwit (*Limosa haemastica*): 15in (38cm)
Far north of North America, wintering in southeastern South America. In the USA it is most commonly sighted on land adjoining the Gulf of Texas each April, during its migration north. Grayish head and neck, and chestnut feathering on underparts. Speckled white plumage on wings, and distinctive black underwing feathering. Long bill is reddish at the base. Hens larger, with whiter underparts.

Whooping crane

Grus americana (E)

Distribution: Restricted areas of Canada and the USA.
Size: 56in (142cm).
Habitat: Peat bog and marshland.
Nest: Flat mound.
Eggs: 2, buff with darker blotches.
Food: Omnivorous.

Standing up to 7½ft (229cm) in height, this is the tallest bird found on the North American continent, as well as one of the most critically endangered. Its breeding grounds are in Wood Buffalo Park, adjoining the Great Slave Lake in Canada. The population moves south in autumn to the wintering grounds at the Arkansas Refuge in Texas. The cranes pause on the long flight to feed on lakes and other similar stretches of water. Their name comes from the distinctive whooping sound of their calls. The graceful dancing display of males is considered one of the most spectacular sights in the natural world. Pairs form a lifelong bond. Nesting usually starts in May.

Identification: Red face and white plumage. The primaries are black, although this may not be very evident when the wings are folded. Sexes are alike. Young birds have a rusty hue, particularly on the head and neck.

RAILS, COOTS AND GALLINULES

Members of this family of waders are most likely to be encountered in relatively shallow stretches of freshwater, particularly where there is dense vegetative cover in the form of reeds. The narrow body shape of these waders helps them to move easily through such terrain, although they also swim quite well. Many species are shy by nature, which can make them difficult to observe.

King rail

Rallus elegans

Distribution: From southern Canada through eastern USA to parts of Mexico. Also present on Cuba and the neighboring Isle of Pines.
Size: 19in (48cm).
Habitat: Freshwater and brackish marshes.
Nest: Cup-shaped.
Eggs: 10–12, creamy buff with purplish-brown spots.
Food: Both plant and animal matter.

Like many of the rails occurring in North America, king rails move south in winter to areas where the temperature is unlikely to drop significantly below freezing, as this would turn their feeding grounds to ice. Aquatic invertebrates feature prominently in their diet, but they are actually omnivorous, eating grass seeds and even fruit, such as blackberries, on occasion. They also prey on frogs and small water snakes. Sadly, in some parts of their range the numbers of king rail have fallen dramatically because of pesticides. Many are killed each year by passing traffic. They can also fall victim to a wide range of predators that may include alligators, raccoons and great horned owls.

Identification: Rusty brown, with darker scalloped patterning over the back and wings. Gray on the ear coverts behind the eyes. Cinnamon underparts with vertical black and white barring on the flanks. Long bill, brown at the tip and orangish further back. Sexes similar but hens are smaller in size.

Giant coot

Fulica gigantea

Occurring in the puna zone of the Andes at altitudes as high as 21,320ft (6,500m), these coots are reputedly not able to fly when adult, although young birds will fly quite readily, often moving down to lakes at lower altitudes for a time. They then return to their traditional haunts for breeding, and have specific nesting requirements. Giant coots construct huge platforms of water weed, often 10ft (3m) or more in length, in the shallows for nesting. The hen lays her eggs in a relatively small, raised cup area, and the same nest site is used and maintained over a number of years. The rim of the nest helps to conceal the chicks once they hatch and protects them from cold winds.

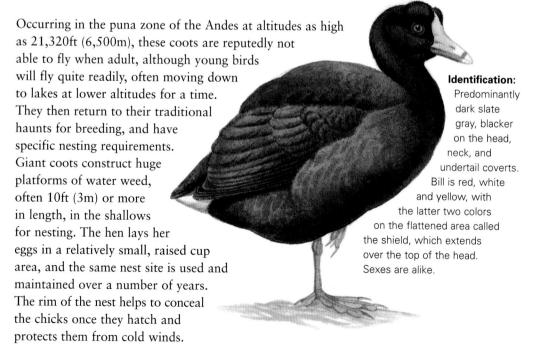

Identification: Predominantly dark slate gray, blacker on the head, neck, and undertail coverts. Bill is red, white and yellow, with the latter two colors on the flattened area called the shield, which extends over the top of the head. Sexes are alike.

Distribution: Central Peru to Bolivia, Chile and north-west Argentina.
Size: 23in (59cm).
Habitat: Shallow lakes and smaller areas of water.
Nest: Large platform built on dense patches of waterweed.
Eggs: 3–7, creamy gray with reddish-brown spots.
Food: Aquatic vegetation.

Clapper rail (*Rallus longirostris*):
16in (41cm)
Mainly coastal areas extending through Mexico
and parts of the Caribbean to northern Peru and
southern Brazil. Grayish sides to the face,
speckled brown back, white throat, with brown
and white barring on the flanks, and white
undertail coverts. Hens are much smaller in size.
Both brown and olive forms are recognized.

Yellow rail (*Coturnicops noveboracensis*):
7in (18cm)
Marshland areas of central and southeastern
parts of Canada to the northeastern USA,
wintering further south in the USA, in Louisiana
and Texas. Brown on top of the head, with a buff
stripe above the eyes, and a brown stripe
running across the eye. Sexes are alike, but
males may be slightly larger.

Sora (Carolina rail, *Porzana carolina*): 10in (25cm)
Freshwater marshland from southeastern Alaska
across much of the USA, sometimes also in
brackish marshes when migrating to South
America. Black area at base of bill, extending
to the forehead, white spot behind the eyes
with grayish coloration on the sides of the face,
merging with barring on the flanks. Upperparts
show dark streaking. Sexes alike.

Gray-necked wood rail (Cayenne wood rail,
Aramides cajanea): 17in (43cm)
Mexico south to parts of Peru, Bolivia, northern
Argentina and Uruguay. Gray area extending from
the head to the upper breast, with orangish-
chestnut coloration on the lower breast. Black
belly and undertail coverts. Upper wing coverts
are greenish olive. Hens are smaller in size.

American coot

Fulica americana

Although there are no striking plumage
differences between the cock and hen, they
can easily be distinguished by a marked
difference in their calls. Unlike some related
species, American coots have proved to be
highly adaptable, to the extent that their
numbers appear to have increased overall in
recent years. They rapidly colonize new areas
of suitable habitat, although populations can
be adversely affected by very cold springtime
weather, which makes food hard to find.
American coots often migrate south in large
numbers to avoid the worst of the winter.

Identification: Predominantly slate gray, more
blackish on the head. White undertail coverts. Bill is
whitish, with red near the tip enlarging into a broad
shield with red at the top. Sexes are alike, although
hens are often significantly smaller.
Young birds predominantly brown,
with duller bills.

Distribution: From Alaska
southward across much of
North America, through
Central America and the
Caribbean into parts
of Colombia.
Size: 17in (43cm).
Habitat: Permanent areas
of wetland.
Nest: Floating heap of dead
aquatic vegetation.
Eggs: 3–12, buff with dense,
fine blackish spotting.
Food: Aquatic vegetation.

Azure gallinule

Little gallinule *Porphyrio flavirostris*

The smallest member of its genus, the azure gallinule
has a discontinuous distribution through South
America. It tends to favor areas of deep
water where there is much vegetation
growing over the surface. In
spite of its long legs, it can
swim if necessary, as well
as sometimes flying up
and perching to escape
danger. Azure gallinules also
use their long legs to climb up
and trample down seeding grasses,
which allows them to extract the seeds.
They are more likely to be seen in
forested areas rather than savanna,
and are known to undertake
seasonal movements.

Identification: Azure plumage
on the wings. The sides of the
head down to the breast are a
bluish gray, and the rest of the
underparts are white. A narrow
band of brown plumage
extends from
the center of
its head down
over the back
and part of the
wings. The bill and
shield are a greenish
yellow. Sexes alike.

Distribution: From Colombia
eastward to French Guiana
and south through Peru to
Bolivia, southern Brazil and
into northern Argentina.
Size: 10in (25cm).
Habitat: Marshland with
good cover.
Nest: Open cup of vegetation.
Eggs: 4–5, creamy with
reddish-brown spots.
Food: Grass seeds
and invertebrates.

LARGER WADERS

*Colorful in some cases and highly adapted to their environments, some larger waders use their bills
as sensory devices, probing for aquatic prey that may be concealed in mud or under loose stones.
The group includes the spoonbills, which have one of the most distinctively shaped bills of all birds.
Many are quite tall, which enables them to spot potential prey over a wide area.*

Scarlet ibis

Eudocimus ruber

The beautiful appearance of these ibises
is derived in part from their diet, which
helps to provide the pigment that
gives them their characteristic
coloration. They live in groups
and comb the mudflats for
crabs and other food
with their stout
but pointed bills.
The scarlet ibis
prefers to nest on
islands, building a
loose nest of sticks
off the ground, often
in mangrove swamps
above the waterline.
This can bring dangers,
however, from crocodiles
that lie in wait, hoping to
seize chicks that have just left
the nest and fall into the water.

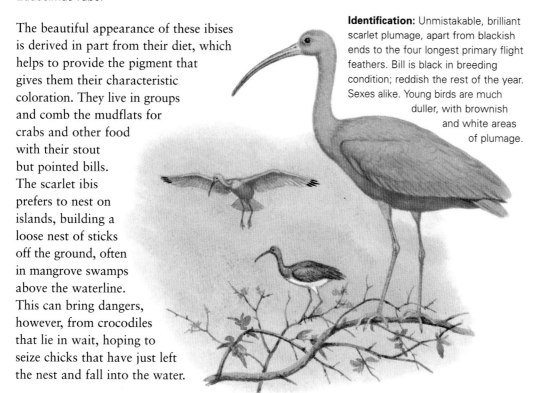

Identification: Unmistakable, brilliant
scarlet plumage, apart from blackish
ends to the four longest primary flight
feathers. Bill is black in breeding
condition; reddish the rest of the year.
Sexes alike. Young birds are much
duller, with brownish
and white areas
of plumage.

Distribution: Concentrated in
northern South America, from
parts of Colombia and
Ecuador through Venezuela
and French Guiana along the
coast of Brazil to the Amazon
Delta. Has reappeared in the
vicinity of São Paulo at
Santos Bay, Brazil.
Size: 27in (69cm).
Habitat: Mangroves,
mudflats and estuaries.
Nest: Sticks and similar
material.
Eggs: 2, pale blue or greenish
with brown blotches.
Food: Crustaceans, small fish
and amphibians.

Whistling heron

Syrigma sibilatrix

Unlike most herons, the whistling heron is often
encountered in areas of wet grassland rather
than in standing water, although it
may be observed in flooded fields
and similar localities. In suitable
areas where food can be found
in abundance, these herons
may congregate in groups
of more than 100 birds,
although they are more
likely to be observed
individually or in pairs.
Their name is derived
from their whistling calls,
which have been likened
to the sound of a flute.

Identification: Rigid black
plumes at the rear of the head.
The face is mainly black, with a
white area under the chin and
a large area of blue skin encircling
the eyes. The neck and breast are
a buff color, becoming paler on
the underparts. The back is
grayish with black edging to the
brownish feathers on each wing.
The legs are fairly dark. The
reddish bill becomes dark at the
tip. Sexes are alike. Young birds
have streaking on the neck.

Distribution: Two distinct
populations in South America:
one in eastern Colombia and
Venezuela; one further south,
extending from Bolivia as far
as southeastern Brazil and
northeastern Argentina.
Size: 24in (61cm).
Habitat: Mainly wet grassland.
Nest: Platform of sticks.
Eggs: 3–4, pale blue
with speckles.
Food: Invertebrates, also
amphibians and reptiles.

Green ibis (*Mesembrinibis cayennensis*): 23in (58cm)
Occurs from eastern Costa Rica and Panama across much of the South American continent, east of the Andes mountain range. Very dark overall with greenish suffusion on the wings and loose greenish plumage at the back of the head. The young lack the gloss on their plumage. Sexes are alike.

Whispering ibis (*Phimosus infuscatus*): 21in (53cm)
Two separate populations: one extends across northern South America from northeast Colombia and eastern Ecuador eastwards; the other occurs south of the Amazon in Brazil, Bolivia, Paraguay, Argentina and Uruguay. Blackish overall, with a bare area of reddish skin on the face. Bill is yellowish, legs are reddish. Sexes are alike.

Buff-necked ibis (*Theristicus caudatus*): 30in (76cm)
Found in Colombia, Venezuela and French Guiana south to northern Argentina and Uruguay. Buff neck, darker on the crown. Mainly gray wings, with a characteristic white area. Buff on the chest, with black underparts. Sexes alike.

Black-crowned night heron (*Nycticorax nycticorax*): 25in (63¹/₂cm)
Central North America through much of South America to Tierra del Fuego. Black back and crown, offset against a whitish face. Wings and tail are gray, and the underparts are white. Short legs. Hens are smaller in size, with shorter head plumes. Young birds are brown.

Sun bittern

Eurypyga helias

The sun bittern has no close relatives and resembles a rail in some respects. It has a relatively long tail, and there is no webbing apparent between its toes. This bird has a fiery, brilliant coloration on the flight feathers and uses these to stunning effect during its mating display. Relatively little is known about the habits of these rather shy birds, which are most likely to be encountered on their own, or sometimes as pairs in damp areas of tropical forest. They use their bills to probe for food in wet areas, but rarely enter the water itself, and they do not fly far.

Identification: Black head with prominent white stripes above and below the eyes, and another white area on the throat. Neck and upperparts are brownish, broken with variable markings ranging from chestnut through gray to black. Orange areas on the wings are most apparent in flight. Dark markings also on the brownish breast, which becomes paler, almost whitish, on the underparts. Bill is straight and yellowish on the upper part. Legs are orangish yellow. Sexes are alike.

Distribution: From southern Mexico south to western Ecuador and east to northern Argentina and Uruguay. Occasionally in Chile.
Size: 19in (48cm).
Habitat: Near streams in wooded areas.
Nest: Globular in shape, made of vegetation and mud.
Eggs: 2, buff with dark spots at the larger end.
Food: Invertebrates.

Roseate spoonbill

Ajaia ajaja

The distinctively enlarged and flattened tips on the spoonbill's beak are very sensitive. They act like a pair of hands, allowing these birds both to detect and grab crabs and similar creatures underwater without difficulty. Roseate spoonbills sometimes immerse their entire head when feeding, although they are more usually observed sweeping their heads from side to side in a characteristic way. These birds are often seen in small flocks on marshland and similar land near coasts. They nest off the ground, building loose piles of sticks.

Identification: Predominantly pink in color, variable in hue, with a more prominent scarlet patch on the shoulders. Has the characteristic spoon-shaped bill and bare greenish skin on the face. Sexes are alike. Young birds are much paler, with whiter areas on head, neck and breast.

Distribution: From southern USA into northern and eastern parts of South America as far south as Argentina. Also occurs in the Caribbean.
Size: 32in (81cm).
Habitat: Wetland areas, typically coastal areas including mangrove swamps.
Nest: Made of sticks.
Eggs: 3, white, brown spots.
Food: Small fish, amphibians and other aquatic creatures.

DUCKS, GEESE AND SWANS

Ducks are a group of waterfowl characterized by their relatively small size compared to swans and geese. They often inhabit stretches of open water, although they are typically quite secretive when nesting. Before the onset of the breeding season, drakes usually molt into much more colorful plumage. For the remainder of the year they have duller, so-called "eclipse" plumage and more closely resemble hens.

Carolina wood duck

American wood duck *Aix sponsa*

Distribution: Occurs widely over much of North America and south to Mexico, being present in western, central and southeastern parts of the continent, as well as on western Cuba.
Size: 20in (51cm).
Habitat: Wooded stretches of freshwater.
Nest: In tree holes.
Eggs: 5–9, buff.
Food: Mainly vegetable matter, from acorns to aquatic plants.

Although these ducks have been seen as far north as Alaska, they move south to a warmer climate for the winter months. In some areas their numbers have benefited from the provision of artificial nesting boxes, so that today they rank among the most common water-fowl in the United States. Carolina wood ducks are likely to be seen dabbling for food in open stretches of water, dipping their heads under the surface, but they also come ashore to nibble at vegetation. Although vagrants sometimes crop up in the Caribbean, Carolina wood ducks observed in other parts of the world will be descendants of escapees from waterfowl collections.

Identification: Crest with glossy green and purple tones in breeding plumage. The lower neck and breast are chestnut with white speckling, while the abdomen is buff with barring on the flanks. Cock resembles the hen in eclipse plumage, but with a more brightly colored bill. The hen is duller in overall coloration, with dark brown underparts.

Muscovy duck

Cairina moschata

These dull-colored waterfowl are far removed in appearance from their more brightly colored domesticated counterparts. They prefer freshwater areas but sometimes move into saltwater lagoons during the dry season. Muscovies live in groups and are arboreal by nature, with powerful claws that help them to climb trees and roost easily on branches. They generally prefer to nest off the ground, but in areas where they are not commonly hunted, hens may lay eggs on the ground in spots that are well camouflaged by surrounding vegetation. The young develop the white wing patches at one year of age.

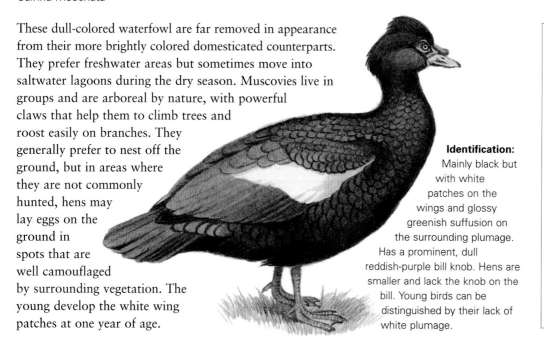

Identification: Mainly black but with white patches on the wings and glossy greenish suffusion on the surrounding plumage. Has a prominent, dull reddish-purple bill knob. Hens are smaller and lack the knob on the bill. Young birds can be distinguished by their lack of white plumage.

Distribution: From Mexico south to parts of Argentina and Uruguay.
Size: 33in (84cm).
Habitat: Forested lakes and marshes.
Nest: Usually in a tree hollow.
Eggs: 8–15, white with greenish suffusion.
Food: Omnivorous.

Hooded merganser

Lophodytes cucullatus

These ducks occur only in small groups of often less than a dozen individuals. They can be difficult to observe, either when resting alongside the water or even when swimming and darting under the surface in search of food. In the far north, hooded mergansers fly south when their freshwater habitat starts to freeze at the onset of winter, often moving to coastal estuaries. They breed off the ground and sometimes nest as high as 80ft (25m) up in suitable trees. They can fly well, displaying great maneuverability at low levels.

Identification: Drakes have a white fan, edged with black, at the rear of the head. The face is black. The chest is white with black-and-white striping behind. The flanks are chestnut, and the back is black. Ducks are mainly brown with a bushy crest. Cocks in eclipse plumage resemble hens but have yellowish rather than brown irises, and darker bills.

Distribution: Two distinct populations, one ranging south from Alaska on the western side of North America. The other extends widely over the east of the continent.
Size: 19in (48cm).
Habitat: Lakes and slow-flowing areas of water near woodland.
Nest: In tree hollows.
Eggs: 6–12, white.
Food: Mainly fish.

Barrow's goldeneye (*Bucephala islandica*): 21in (53cm)
Separate populations in western and eastern North America, also present on Greenland and Iceland. Dark green glossy head, with a white patch in front of each eye, and mainly white underparts. Cocks in eclipse plumage have black bills and retain the black-and-white barring on the sides of the wings. Hens are darker and duller, with a distinctive golden eye.

Ruddy duck (*Oxyura jamaicensis*): 17in (43cm)
Occurs across much of North America and down the west side of South America. Broad bill and upright tail feathers. Chestnut-brown coloration (replaced by brown in eclipse plumage), with black and usually white plumage on the head. Some regional variations in appearance. Hens are predominantly brown.

Whistling swan (tundra swan, *Cygnus columbianus*): 58in (147cm)
Breeds in the Arctic, with wintering populations in western and eastern USA. White, with small yellow patch sometimes evident on blackish bill. Sexes alike, but males may be larger. Young birds are grayer, with more reddish-orange bills.

Ross's goose (*Anser rossii*): 26in (66cm)
Breeds in the far north of central Canada, near the Perry River, wintering in the southwest USA and along the Mexican border. Occurs in both snow (white) and blue phases, like its relative, the snow goose (*A. caerulescens*), retaining the white plumage on the head in its blue phase. Sexes are alike, but males are often larger.

American wigeon

Anas americana

These wigeon are sometimes seen well outside their normal range, with reports of sightings in locations as far apart as Hawaii, the Komandorskie islands off Siberia and Europe. Almost every year a few vagrant American wigeon are recorded by birdwatchers in the British Isles. The ability of these ducks to cross the Atlantic Ocean is all the more surprising because they are essentially vegetarian in their feeding habits, browsing on plants in and out of the water. A number of American wigeon also migrate south each year to South America, and are observed there in larger numbers outside the breeding season.

Distribution: Much of North America, including the far north. Often moves southward in winter.
Size: 22in (59cm).
Habitat: Freshwater marshland.
Nest: In a hollow often hidden in grass, lined with down feathers.
Eggs: 6–12, creamy white.
Food: Aquatic vegetation, small aquatic invertebrates.

Identification: In breeding condition, a prominent white stripe extends back over the top of the head, with a broad dark green area incorporating the eyes, and speckling beneath. The remainder of the plumage is brownish with a white belly and broader white area on the lower body close to the tail. Ducks have completely speckled heads and lack the drake's white forewing, which is retained in the eclipse plumage. The duck has paler chestnut coloration than the drake in eclipse plumage.

COTINGAS

The cotingas include some of the most colorful of all tropical birds, although their name comes from an Amazonian native American word meaning "washed white," which is used locally to describe the white bellbird. Their diet consists mainly of fruits and berries, and this group of birds is important in the dispersal of plants—undigested seeds from their food are passed onto the ground.

Scarlet cock-of-the-rock

Andean cock-of-the-rock *Rupicola peruviana*

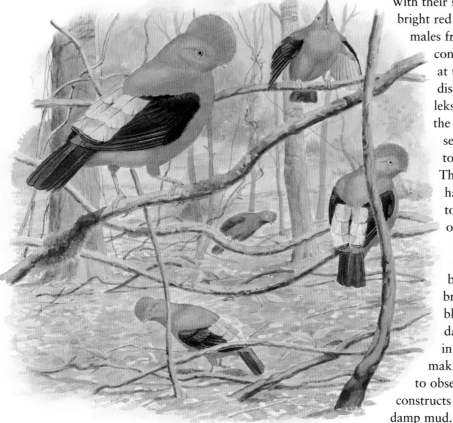

With their spectacular bright red plumage, males frequently congregate together at traditional displays sites called leks, often deep in the forest. Here they seek to entice hens to mate with them. Their display calls have been likened to the squealing of pigs, although these cotingas are not noisy by nature. Their brilliant plumage blends into the dark background in the forest, making them hard to observe. The hen constructs her nest using damp mud.

Distribution: Colombia and Venezuela to parts of Ecuador, Peru and Bolivia.
Size: 12½in (32cm).
Habitat: Humid, rocky areas of forest, often in ravines close to water.
Nest: Cup made of mud, located in a secluded rocky outcrop or cave.
Eggs: 2, buff with darker spotting.
Food: Mainly berries and other fruit.

Identification: Brilliant red dominates in the plumage, with crest feathers extending down over the bill, contrasting with black on the back and wings. Hens are significantly duller in color, and are generally reddish brown with a smaller crest.

Fiery-throated fruiteater

Pipreola chlorolepidota

This is the smallest of the Andean fruiteaters. It is found at a lower altitude than related species, typically less than 3,280ft (1,000m) above sea level, in the foothills of the Andes. These members of the cotinga clan are most likely to be observed singly or in pairs. They may breed throughout the year, building a moss nest lined with small roots, usually close to the ground and often disguised in a creeper. The fiery-throated fruiteater is unusual in that it does venture up into the canopy of the forest, although it is also commonly seen in the lower levels, often seeking food in the company of other birds.

Identification: The underparts are dark green, with a yellowish-orange throat area; remainder of the plumage is also green. Bill is reddish. Hens closely resemble female scarlet-breasted fruiteater (*P. frontalis*), being predominantly green, with yellow barring extending from the throat over all of the underparts.

Distribution: Eastern areas of Ecuador and Peru.
Size: 4in (10cm).
Habitat: Humid tropical forest.
Nest: Cup-shaped.
Eggs: Probably 2, creamy and spotted.
Food: Mainly berries and other fruit, also invertebrates.

Orange cock-of-the-rock (Guianan cock-of-the-rock, *Rupicola rupicola*): 12½in (32cm)
Found in Guyana, Surinam and French Guiana west to Colombia, and also in northern Brazil. Unmistakable shade of brilliant orange. The hen is mainly olive brown with an orange suffusion on the rump.

Pompadour cotinga (*Xipholena punicea*): 8in (20cm)
Extends from Colombia, eastward to French Guiana and south to northwestern Brazil. Wine-red plumage with white areas on the wings. Hens are gray, with white edging to some wing feathers. The eyes are whitish.

Plum-throated cotinga (*Cotinga maynana*): 7½in (19cm)
Ranges from southeastern Colombia to northern Bolivia and Amazonian Brazil. Turquoise with a small plum-colored throat patch. Hens are brown with pale edges to the feathers. They have cinnamon plumage on the lower abdomen.

Barred fruiteater (*Pipreola arcuata*): 8½in (22cm)
Found in Andean region of western South America at altitudes of 10,500ft (3,200m) in cloud forest. Blackish head, with barring confined to the chest and underparts, which are green in hens.

Red-crested cotinga (*Ampelion rubrocristatus*): 9in (23cm)
Found in the Andean region of Colombia and western Venezuela south to northern Bolivia. Grayish brown, with a blacker tone on the head, back and wings. Reddish crest at the back of the head is often kept flat. Undertail coverts are streaked with white. White areas on the underside of the tail. Bill is white with a black tip. Iris is red. Sexes are alike.

Long-wattled umbrellabird

Cephalopterus penduliger

As the name suggests, the male of this species has a bizarre black-feathered wattle extending down from his chest that measures approximately 12in (30cm) long. It is inflated as part of his display, but shortened during flight and held close to the chest. The flight pattern of umbrellabirds is not dissimilar to that of woodpeckers, low and strong over the trees. Quiet by nature, solitary and rarely observed, males are most likely to be seen displaying on bare branches, when their booming calls are uttered. These calls are heard with increasing frequency during the nesting season, although it appears that the hen alone is responsible for rearing the offspring.

Identification:
Predominantly black in color. Very long wattle, which is greatly reduced in females. Both have relatively small crests. Brown eyes help to distinguish these cotingas from related umbrellabirds.

Distribution: Western Colombia and north-western Ecuador.
Size: 20in (51cm) cock; 18in (46cm) hen.
Habitat: Lowland tropical forest.
Nest: Platform of twigs.
Eggs: 1, khaki colored.
Food: Mainly palm fruits and insects.

Purple-breasted cotinga

Cotinga cotinga

One of the most striking features of these cotingas is their small yet broad bills, which allow them to pluck and swallow quite large fruits whole. They belong to the group often known as the blue cotingas, so called because of the predominant color of the cock bird. Individuals are most likely to be seen perching on dead treetops, although they fly with a strange rattling noise, which is thought to be caused by the modified shape of their flight feathers. Little is known about their breeding habits, but it is believed that hens incubate and rear their chicks on their own.

Identification:
Silhouette is like that of a dove. Distinctive reddish-purple feathering from the throat down to the middle of the belly; the remainder of the body is violet blue, apart from the black wings and tail. Small yet broad bill. Hens are dark brown, with white edging to the feathers, creating a scaly appearance over the whole body.

Distribution: Eastern Colombia to French Guiana and Brazil.
Size: 7½in (19cm).
Habitat: Lowland tropical forest.
Nest: Small, flimsy and cup-shaped.
Eggs: Probably 1–2, bluish with rusty-brown markings.
Food: Primarily fruit.

QUETZALS, TROGONS AND JACAMARS

Quetzals have a special mythical significance in ancient South American culture and feature prominently in Mayan legend and symbolism. Trogons as a group have a much wider distribution overall, with relatives in Africa. Jacamars are mainly found in South rather than Central America, and are characterized by their slim body shape, long tail and narrow bill.

Crested quetzal

Pharomachrus antisianus

Distribution: Colombia and western Venezuela to Brazil in the east and southward as far as Bolivia.
Size: 13in (33cm).
Habitat: Humid forest. Typically occurs in cloud forest in the Andean region up to an altitude of about 9,840ft (3,000m).
Nest: Tree holes or termite nests.
Eggs: 2, light blue.
Food: Berries, other fruit and also invertebrates.

Quetzals have a distinctive, upright stance when perching, when they rest so quietly that they are easily overlooked. They are most likely to be seen close to fruiting trees on which they feed. These quetzals have an undulating flight pattern, and their calls are a loud sequence of rolling notes. The plumage of crested quetzals, like that of related species, is brightly colored but fades quite rapidly after death, so museum specimens rarely display the vibrancy of living birds. Another unusual feature is their very thin skin.

Identification: Distinguished from other quetzals by the white undersides to the tail feathers; hens have barred feathering here. The hen can also be distinguished from the cock by her brown rather than green head, and a reduced area of red on the underparts. Young birds resemble the female.

White-tailed trogon

Trogon viridis

Like other trogons, the white-tailed type may be sedentary for long periods, but is sufficiently agile to feed on fruit in flight, as well as to catch invertebrates on the wing. These trogons will also swoop on small vertebrate prey, such as lizards. The bill is short, but has a wide gape to facilitate swallowing. Their perching grip is unusual too, with two toes being directed in front of and behind the perch, rather than the more usual 3:1 perching configuration. In common with other trogons, they do not build a nest, but the hens simply lay their eggs in a suitable chamber. They have even been known to use a termite nest, and the presence of termites deters would-be predators. Here the nesting chamber is a hollow, constructed at the end of a tunnel that usually leads in an upwardly diagonal direction.

Identification: Glossy violet feathering from the head to the chest. Yellow underparts and a dark green back, with a distinctive, mainly white underside to the tail. Blue eye rings. Bill is bluish white. The hen is duller in appearance, slate-colored with orangish-yellow underparts and a dusky upper bill.

Distribution: Costa Rica and Panama south to Colombia, Ecuador, Peru and Brazil. Also on Trinidad.
Size: 11in (28cm).
Habitat: Humid forest.
Nest: Usually in a tree hole.
Eggs: 2, light blue.
Food: Berries, other fruit and some invertebrates.

Pavonine quetzal (*Pharomachrus pavoninus*): 13in (33cm)
This is the only quetzal found east of the Andes mountains, ranging south to northern Bolivia. Distinctive red bill and red lower underparts, otherwise the plumage is a metallic shade of emerald green. The hen is less colorful and has a black underside to the tail.

Black-throated trogon (*Trogon rufus*): 10in (25cm)
Ranges from southeastern Honduras down to Paraguay and northeastern Argentina. Distinctive green-and-yellow coloration, separated on the chest by a thin white band. The hen is distinguished from the cock by her brown and yellow feathering.

White-eared jacamar (*Galbalcyrhynchus leucotis*): 8in (20cm)
Restricted to the northern part of the Upper Amazonian region. Recognizable by its large, pinkish bill and white areas of plumage behind the eyes. Reddish-chestnut overall with dark wings. Sexes are alike.

Striped manakin (*Machaeropterus regulus*): 3½in (9cm)
Extends from northwestern South America, from Colombia and Venezuela south to Peru, Bolivia and Brazil, occurring in the Andes at altitudes of up to 4,900ft (1,500m). Brilliant red cap, with reddish streaking on the undersides of the body. The hen is a dull shade of green overall, and is paler and yellower on the underparts, with a white underside to the tail feathers. There are also darker streaks on the sides of the body, with a rufous hue on the flanks.

Paradise jacamar

Galbula dea

The jacamars form a group closely related to woodpeckers, and are members of the avian order Piciformes (which includes woodpeckers and trogons). Like trogons, they have a zygodactyl perching grip, with two toes directed forward over the perch and two behind. In common with related species, the paradise jacamar has a long, thin bill. It hunts insects on the wing, using its bill to grab prey in flight. These are not especially shy birds, and are most likely to be seen either in pairs or small parties in forest clearings or sometimes when swooping out across water. Their call note is a distinctive "pip" sound that is repeated frequently. These jacamars, unlike other species, often remain in the tree canopy, where they are difficult to observe, thanks in part to their coloration. Paradise jacamars will often accompany groups of other birds, seizing any invertebrates that are disturbed as a result of the other birds' movements.

Identification: Distinctive dark body and a long tail that tapers along its length. White feathering under the throat and dark, glossy green wings. Bill is long and black. Sexes alike. The color of the crown may be either pale gray or dark brown, depending on the race.

Distribution: Northern South America to parts of Brazil, Peru and Bolivia.
Size: 12in (30cm).
Habitat: Occurs in forest and more open country.
Nest: May excavate into the mounds of arboreal termites or a suitable bank.
Eggs: 2–4, glossy white.
Food: Invertebrates.

Golden-winged manakin

Masius chrysopterus

These small birds are most likely to be spotted flying through the understorey in forests, sometimes heading up into the canopy in search of fruit. Golden-winged manakins normally seek out berries, which they can pluck on the wing, as well as invertebrates, which figure more prominently in their diet during the breeding period when there are chicks in the nest. Little is known of their habits, but they appear to be relatively solitary by nature. Males use their bright wing coloration for display purposes.

Identification: Distinctive golden-yellow edging to the wings and a yellow crest on the forehead, with this color extending onto the throat and back over the head, where it becomes orangish. The remainder of the plumage is glossy black. Hen is greenish, but with prominent yellow feathering in the vicinity of the chin and belly.

Distribution: In the Andean region of Colombia to Venezuela, Ecuador and Peru.
Size: 4in (10cm).
Habitat: Cloud forest and woodland.
Nest: Suspended cup-shape, made of moss and rootlets.
Eggs: 2, cream with brown spots.
Food: Berries and some invertebrates.

TOUCANS, ARACARIS AND TOUCANETS

Members of the toucan clan are virtually unmistakable, although not all of them have large, brightly colored bills. Active and restless by nature, they often congregate in large numbers in fruiting trees, hopping from branch to branch. When roosting and breeding in tree holes where their bills could be an encumbrance, they pull their tail feathers up vertically and tuck their bills over their backs.

Crimson-rumped toucanet

Aulacorhynchus haematopygus

The term "toucanet" is applied to smaller members of this family, with green predominating in the plumage of all six *Aulacorhynchus* species. These toucanets are active and quite noisy birds, hopping from branch to branch in search of food. Eating is a two-stage process. Fruit is plucked and then skilfully tossed up into the air and swallowed whole. Pits (stones) are regurgitated later. Larger items can be held against the perch with the foot, allowing chunks to be torn off and then eaten in a similar way. The zygodactyl arrangement of these birds' toes, with two toes directed forward and two behind the perch, helps them to hold their food securely.

Identification: Predominantly green, darker on the wings with distinctive red plumage over the rump. Dark, reddish-brown bill, with white at the base and prominent dull reddish skin encircling the eyes. Sexes alike.

Distribution: Colombia, Venezuela and Ecuador.
Size: 16in (41cm).
Habitat: Humid forest and secondary woodland.
Nest: Tree hollow.
Eggs: 3–4, white.
Food: Fruit, small vertebrates and invertebrates. May also steal eggs and chicks.

Toco toucan

Ramphastos toco

Distribution: Guyana, Surinam and French Guiana south to Brazil, Paraguay, Bolivia and northern Argentina.
Size: 21in (53cm).
Habitat: Unusual in ranging from forest to savanna. On rare occasions, large flocks have moved into towns where ripening fruit is plentiful nearby.
Nest: Hollow in tree, sometimes previously occupied by woodpeckers.
Eggs: 2, white.
Food: Berries other fruit and invertebrates. Also raids nests of other birds.

Just why toucans have such large, brightly colored bills is something of a mystery. These lightweight, honeycombed structures contain a long, fringed tongue. Its function is unknown, but it probably helps these toucans to swallow food. It is thought that the bill may enable these birds to pluck fruits that would otherwise be out of their reach at the end of thin branches. The bright colors set against their subdued plumage may also be a useful defensive aid, and certainly, the serrated edges of the bill can inflict a painful wound. Toco toucans are less social by nature than other members of the family, although they may congregate in large groups in areas where food is plentiful. They have a call that has been likened to the sound of deep snoring.

Identification: Largest of the toucans. Glossy black plumage with prominent white bib on the throat and red around the vent. Bare area of bright blue skin around the eyes, with small area of surrounding yellow feathering. Large, broad bill displaying shades of yellow and yellowish-orange coloration, black at the base, with a prominent black tip to the upper bill. Sexes are alike.

Lettered aracari

Pteroglossus inscriptus

These aracaris get their name from the traces on their upper bill, which look like lettering. Aracaris are social by nature, and are most likely to be observed in groups. It is thought that in some cases, the young of the previous year may remain with their parents and assist in the rearing of the following year's young. The chicks hatch with heel pads that help them to keep their balance, although their bills at this time are relatively small. These pads fall off once the young birds have left the nest. Aracaris and other toucans rely on an adequate number of tree holes for breeding purposes because, unlike woodpeckers, their bills are not strong enough to allow them to bore effectively into trees.

Identification: The lack of banding across the yellow feathering of the chest is distinctive. Upperparts are greenish. Traces similar to letters on the upper bill, whereas lower bill is mainly black. Sexes alike.

Distribution: Eastern Colombia to central and southern Brazil, and into northern Bolivia.
Size: 14½in (37cm).
Habitat: Forested areas and more open woodland.
Nest: Tree holes.
Eggs: 2–3, white.
Food: Berries, other fruit, invertebrates and small vertebrates.

Red-billed toucan (*Ramphastos tucanus*): 24in (61cm)
Occurs in Venezuela to French Guiana into parts of Brazil and eastern Bolivia. Dark reddish sides to the bill, yellow on top, with a white chest and red band beneath. Predominantly black plumage elsewhere, although the vent area is red. Sexes are alike.

Sulphur-breasted toucan (keel-billed toucan, *Ramphastos sulfuratus*): 19in (48cm)
Found in Central America, from southern Mexico to northern Colombia and Venezuela. Bill is pea-green with orange stripe on upper part. Brilliant yellow plumage on the chest, predominantly black elsewhere. Sexes are alike.

Golden-collared toucanet (*Selenidera reinwardtii*): 13in (33cm)
Found in southern parts of Colombia, extending to parts of Ecuador, Peru and Brazil. Bill is a deep shade of red with a black tip. Plumage is mainly black and green, with a yellow collar and ear flashes. Hen has rufous coloration, not black.

Spot-billed toucanet (*Selenidera maculirostris*): 13in (33cm)
Confined to Brazil. Predominantly ivory bill with black markings. Mainly black head and chest, whereas the hen has reddish-brown plumage here. Lower underparts are yellowish.

Many-banded aracari (*Pteroglossus pluricinctus*): 17in (43cm)
From Colombia and Venezuela south to northern Peru and Brazil. Black apart from ivory area down the sides of the upper bill. Two black bands run across the underparts, which are pale yellow with reddish markings. Upperparts are dark. Blue skin around the eyes. Rump is red. Sexes are alike.

Plate-billed mountain toucan

Andigena laminirostris

The four species of mountain toucan are all found at relatively high altitudes, and can be distinguished from the *Ramphastos* genus by their smaller bills. The plate-billed mountain toucan is so-called because of the presence of raised yellowish patches on each side of the beak. The function of these is unclear. Blue features prominently in the coloration of all mountain toucans, and the plumage is soft and quite loose. The wings of these toucans have the typical rounded shape associated with other members of the family, which means that they do not fly especially powerfully.

Identification: Characteristic yellow plate on each side of the upper bill, with black elsewhere and dull reddish base. Dark, sky-blue plumage on the underparts, with black cap on the head extending down the neck. Wings are olive brown. Sexes are alike.

Distribution: Colombia and western parts of Ecuador.
Size: 20in (51cm).
Habitat: Humid and wet mountain forests.
Nest: Tree hollow.
Eggs: 2–3, white.
Food: Berries, other fruit, invertebrates and small vertebrates.

Left: Toucans roost and nest in tree holes.

BARBETS, BELLBIRDS, FRUITCROWS AND PUFFBIRDS

These birds are typical inhabitants of tropical forest. Barbets are also well represented in Africa, whereas bellbirds and fruitcrows are confined to America. Like other fruit-eating species, they have an important role in helping to spread the seeds of the plants on which they feed. Puffbirds, in contrast, feed on invertebrates and even on small vertebrates. They, too, occur only in America.

Toucan barbet

Semnornis ramphastinus

Distribution: Western parts of Colombia and Ecuador. Typically between 3,280 and 7,870ft (1,000 and 2,400m).
Size: 8in (20cm).
Habitat: Humid mountain forests.
Nest: Tree hollow.
Eggs: 2, white.
Food: Berries, other fruit and invertebrates.

The coloration of these barbets is not dissimilar to that of mountain toucans, which is how they got their name. Their bills, in contrast, are both stocky and powerful, enabling them to bore into wood to create or enlarge a nest in a tree hollow. Their tails are flexible, and can be carried either down or raised into a more vertical position. The toucan barbet's range is relatively restricted, and it tends not to be common, with just odd birds or pairs being sighted rather than groups. Like many barbets, they can call loudly, with members of a pair taking part in a duet of loud honking notes with each other. Calling of this type is most common during the nesting season.

Identification: Prominent bluish-gray area on the sides of the face and chest. Orangish-red underparts, becoming more yellowish toward the vent, with an olive-brown back and yellowish rump. Wings and tail are bluish-gray. Bill is tipped with black. Sexes are alike.

Five-colored barbet

Capito quinticolor

These barbets are not perhaps as colorful as their name might suggest. They have a localized distribution on the western (Pacific) side of the Andes, and they are not especially easy to observe, often occurring just as individuals hopping through the vegetation, or in pairs. They sometimes associate with other birds, possibly hoping to snatch invertebrates that may be disturbed as the flock moves from tree to tree. Five-colored barbets do not range up into the mountains, but are found in lowland areas, at altitudes of 330ft (100m) or below.

Identification: Distinctive yellow V-shape at the top of the mainly black wings. The chest is predominantly white. Underparts are yellowish orange, with black spotting on the flanks, and olive thighs. Hens have streaked upperparts and spotted underparts, and lack the crimson crown and nape seen in cocks.

Distribution: Restricted to western parts of Colombia, extending from Quibdó, Tadó and Chocó southward along the Pacific coast as far down as western Nariño.
Size: 7in (18cm).
Habitat: Forested areas of the coastal lowlands.
Nest: Cavity in a tree.
Eggs: 3, white.
Food: Berries, other fruit and invertebrates.

Red-headed barbet (*Eubucco bourcierii*):
6½in (16½cm)
Ranges from Costa Rica and Panama south to
Colombia and Ecuador. Only cocks have red heads—
those of hens are grayish. Rest of the plumage is
greenish and striped on the underparts.

Prong-billed barbet (*Semnornis frantzii*):
7in (18cm)
Confined to western Panama and Costa Rica, where
this barbet is more common. Olive-green upperparts
with buff coloration on the upper breast. Crown is
a dull, golden-brown shade, with a raised crest
of glossy black feathers at the back of the head.
Lower bill is divided, with the tip of the upper bill
lying in the notch created where the two halves
join. Hens are easily distinguished from cocks by
the lack of black feathering.

White-necked puffbird (*Notharchus
macrorhynchus*): 10in (25cm)
The five recognized races of these puffbirds have
a wide distribution, ranging from Mexico south to
parts of Paraguay and northeastern Argentina. This
species is also found in Brazil, Guyana, Surinam and
French Guiana. White on the forehead, chest
and abdomen. Black elsewhere, in a band across the
chest, around the eyes and on the wings. Barred on
the sides of the body. Sexes are alike.

Spotted puffbird (*Bucco tamatia*): 7in (18cm)
Northern South America, from Colombia, Venezuela
to French Guiana south through Ecuador to Peru and
east into Brazil. Cinnamon plumage across the
throat, black-and-white barring beneath, with a black
bar on the lower cheeks. Sexes are alike.

Bare-throated bellbird

Procnias nudicollis

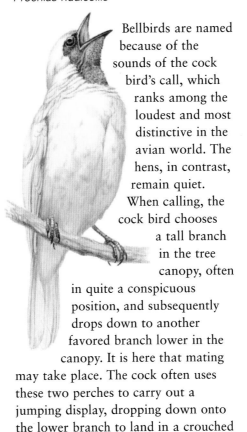

Bellbirds are named
because of the
sounds of the cock
bird's call, which
ranks among the
loudest and most
distinctive in the
avian world. The
hens, in contrast,
remain quiet.
When calling, the
cock bird chooses
a tall branch
in the tree
canopy, often
in quite a conspicuous
position, and subsequently
drops down to another
favored branch lower in the
canopy. It is here that mating
may take place. The cock often uses
these two perches to carry out a
jumping display, dropping down onto
the lower branch to land in a crouched
position with his tail feathers spread.
Studies on this species have revealed
that bare-throated bellbirds move
seasonally, descending to lower altitudes
outside the breeding season.

Distribution: Southern Brazil,
northeastern Argentina
and Paraguay.
Size: 9½in (24cm).
Habitat: Montane forest.
Nest: Light and bowl-shaped,
often in a tree fork.
Eggs: 1, light tan with
brown mottling.
Food: Almost exclusively
frugivorous, feeding on
berries and other fruit.

Identification: Snowy-white
feathering, with blackish bill and
feet, plus a bare bluish-green
area under the throat extending
just around the eyes. Contrasting
dark irises, bill and legs. The
cock's calls are made by the
syrinx, located in the throat.
Hens are strikingly different,
with a dark head, green wings
and yellow-streaked underparts,
which become yellower on the
lower abdomen. Young birds
develop their bare throats by the
time they are one year old.

Purple-throated fruitcrow

Querula purpurata

Like bellbirds, these are cotingas, not corvids as their
common name might suggest. Purple-throated
fruitcrows are not active birds by nature, which means
they can be easily overlooked in forested areas. They are
most conspicuous either when in flight or feeding,
especially when they dart out quickly to seize berries or
feed in the company of other frugivorous birds such as
trogons. These fruitcrows live in groups of three or four
individuals, and although only the female incubates, all
members of the group provide
food for the young bird.
When displaying,
males inflate their
purple gorget of
feathers, which then
resembles a shield.

*Left: The fruitcrow's nest may be
at least 70ft (22m) off the ground.*

Distribution: Costa Rica and
Panama south to Amazonian
region of Brazil and
northern Bolivia.
Size: 11in (28cm).
Habitat: Tropical forest.
Nest: Cup-shaped, relatively
high off the ground.
Eggs: 1, blackish.
Food: Berries, other fruits
and invertebrates.

Identification: Predominantly black, with a distinctive area of purplish
plumage under the throat. Hens are entirely black in color, as are young
birds of both sexes. The tail is quite short, with rounded wings.

CRACIDS, TINAMOUS AND GROUND BIRDS

There are a number of relatively large birds represented in America. The curassows, guans and chachalacas together form the family Cracidae. They tend to be more arboreal than the tinamous, which form a separate group. Antpittas and trumpeters are primarily ground-dwelling birds from this region, and they live and feed mainly on the forest floor.

Great tinamou

Tinamus major

Approximately 40 different species of tinamou occur from Mexico to the tip of South America. Like others of its kind, the great tinamou is difficult to observe, in spite of its size. These birds rarely fly unless there is danger close by, and they move quite quietly through the forest, where their coloration helps them to merge into the background. Their call consists of whistling notes, sometimes heard after dark. The nest is always well concealed in thick, inaccessible vegetation. The cock bird is believed to be largely responsible for incubating the eggs. The eggs themselves can vary quite widely in color, even being violet in some cases. The chicks are able to move readily within a day of hatching. Their flight feathers grow rapidly, so that the young birds can fly when they are little bigger than a robin.

Identification: Large, plump appearance. Grayish-brown underparts, with a more olive hue across the back. White areas on throat, with chestnut feathering on the crown in many cases. Sexes alike but hens may be larger. Young birds are darker in color than adults.

Distribution: From Mexico south to parts of Ecuador, Peru and Brazil, with approximately a dozen different subspecies being found throughout the area up to about 3,280ft (1,000m).
Size: 18in (46cm).
Habitat: Generally lowland areas in humid forests.
Nest: Leaf-lined scraping on the ground, often disguised in buttress roots.
Eggs: 6–7, glossy turquoise ranging to violet.
Food: Berries, seeds and invertebrates.

Andean guan

Penelope montagnii

These large birds are primarily arboreal by nature, living in groups of three to six individuals outside the breeding season. They tend to be encountered at higher altitudes than other guans, certainly in Colombia where they have been observed up to 10,500ft (3,500m). They sometimes leave the cover of dense forest in search of fruit, venturing into isolated trees where such food is plentiful. They usually forage in the branches, however, rather than on the ground. Andean guans have a loud honking call, which is heard more frequently during the breeding period. These birds have been heavily hunted, like related species, are shy, and avoid areas near human settlements.

Identification: Brownish overall, with grayish markings on the plumage extending from the head down to the breast. A small area of bare red skin forms the dewlap, which is often hard to observe from a distance, and the throat is more feathered than in other guans. Legs are reddish. Sexes are alike.

Distribution: In the Andean region of Colombia, north-west Venezuela, Ecuador, Peru and Bolivia. This species may extend as far south as northwestern parts of Argentina, although it is doubtful.
Size: 24in (61cm).
Habitat: Forested areas at relatively high altitudes.
Nest: Platform of leaves and twigs.
Eggs: 1–3, white.
Food: Berries, other fruit and seeds.

Gray-winged trumpeter

Common trumpeter *Psophia crepitans*

Distribution: Northwestern South America eastward through French Guiana.
Size: 24in (61cm).
Habitat: Rainforest.
Nest: Leaf-lined tree cavity.
Eggs: 6, white.
Food: Fruits, plant matter and invertebrates.

Trumpeters are commonly seen walking together in small groups, and are easily tamed if obtained young. They make useful watchdogs, uttering loud grunts as warning calls. They are also valued for their snake-killing abilities, and these reptiles may feature as part of their natural diet. The plumage on the head and neck is short and has a velvety texture. Their overall appearance resembles that of miniature rheas, although trumpeters retain four toes on each foot. Their legs are powerful, allowing them not just to run but also swim effectively. Trumpeters spend most of their time on the ground, although they prefer to roost in trees when not active after dark.

Identification: Plumage predominantly black, with purplish feathering at the base of the neck. The plumage on the head is very short and has a plush texture. Gray coloration is apparent on the wings. Upright stance. Sexes are alike.

Great curassow

Crax rubra

Distribution: Mexico southwards to Colombia and Ecuador.
Size: 36in (91cm).
Habitat: Lowland forest.
Nest: Platform off the ground.
Eggs: 2, rough-shelled, white.
Food: Plant matter.

The curassows tend to be more terrestrial than other cracids, although they invariably roost off the ground. Pairs also nest off the ground, sometimes at heights of up to 100ft (30m) in a suitable tree. Great curassows are most likely to be encountered individually or in pairs, rather than in larger groups. Cocks of this species have a deep, booming call and also utter high-pitched whistling notes. Their range has contracted in some areas, such as along the Pacific coast of Colombia, because of the combined effect of overhunting and deforestation. In areas where great curassows are not persecuted, these large birds can be quite conspicuous.

Identification: Mainly black, with a white abdomen and undertail coverts. Striking yellow knob on the upper bill, which is absent in hens and immatures. Hens are mainly chestnut, but with black-and-white barring on the head and neck. Those from Central America may be darker and display more barring.

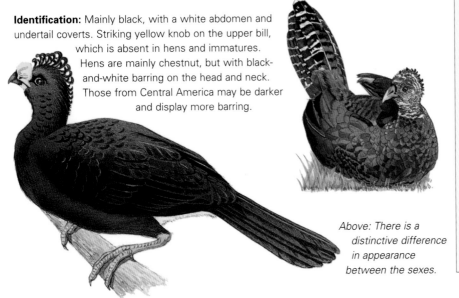

Above: There is a distinctive difference in appearance between the sexes.

Plain chachalaca (*Ortalis vetula*):
25in (63½cm)
Southern Texas in the USA south to Mexico and Nicaragua, as well as the Honduran island of Utila. Predominantly brownish, with bare, blue skin on the face and flesh-colored throat. Relatively noisy and quite adaptable by nature, in the face of primary deforestation. Sexes alike.

Band-tailed guan (*Penelope argyrotis*):
26in (66cm)
Found in parts of Venezuela and Colombia. Large red dewlap under the throat and frosty white plumage on the sides of the head. Has a distinctive pale tail band not seen in other guans, and also has a stocky appearance compared with related guans. Predominantly brown with white streaking on the breast and mantle. Sexes are alike.

Wattled curassow (*Crax globulosa*):
35in (89cm)
Southeastern Colombia south to northern Bolivia and the western upper Amazonian region of Brazil. Predominantly black with a curly crest. Two distinctive red wattles at the base of the lower mandible, with a similar knob on the top of the bill at its base. These swellings are sometimes yellowish. Sometimes a marbled plumage patterning is evident over the wings. Hens have no wattles or knob, and have a white rather than chestnut belly and undertail coverts.

Giant antpitta (*Grallaria gigantea*):
10½in (27cm)
Occurs in parts of Colombia and Ecuador, and lives on the forest floor. Reddish brown with black barring on the underparts. Olive-brown upperparts and grayish suffusion on the head. Sexes are alike.

MACAWS

The macaws include the largest and most spectacular members of the entire parrot family. All 17 species are characterized by their long tails and the prominent, largely unfeathered areas of skin on their faces. Their distribution ranges from Central America through to the southern parts of South America.

Blue and gold macaw

Blue and yellow macaw *Ara ararauna*

Distribution: Eastern Panama and Colombia south through Amazonia to southeastern Brazil, Bolivia and Paraguay.
Size: 30–33in (76–84cm).
Habitat: Forested areas near water.
Nest: Tall hollow tree.
Eggs: 2, white.
Food: Nuts, fruits and seeds.

Wooded areas are the normal habitat of these colorful macaws, which usually feed in the treetops. Their presence there is revealed by their loud, raucous calls, which are also uttered when the birds are in flight. Although normally observed in pairs or small family groups, blue and gold macaws do form larger flocks, consisting of up to 25 individuals on occasion. They are most likely to be observed during the morning and again at dusk, as they fly back and forth between their roosting and feeding sites. One of the main factors restricting the distribution of these macaws is the availability of suitable palms as nesting sites. They are quite adaptable in their feeding habits, eating a wide variety of plant matter and even sometimes seeking nectar from flowers.

Identification: Predominantly blue upperparts, with contrasting golden-yellow underparts. Greenish area on the forehead above the bill. Bare, unfeathered white skin on the sides of the face, with small tracts of black feathers here and a black band beneath the throat. Sexes alike. The rare Bolivian blue-throated macaw (*A. glaucogularis*) is similar in its overall coloration, but can be distinguished by its prominent blue cheek patches.

Red and green macaw

Green-winged macaw *Ara chloroptera*

As in related species, these large macaws display isolated feather tracts across the bare areas of skin on each side of their face. Rather like fingerprints, this feature is sufficiently distinctive to enable individuals to be identified at close quarters. Young birds display odd maroon rather than crimson feathers here, and also have dark eyes. Adult pairs remain together throughout the year, although they may not breed annually. They can live for more than 50 years. Red and green macaws usually feed in the canopy, and are sometimes seen there in the company of blue and gold macaws. These parrots are able to use their feet like hands to grasp their food. Pairs frequently engage in mutual preening when resting in trees during the hottest part of the day.

Identification: Rich crimson feathering predominates, with both bluish and distinctive green feathering evident on the lower part of the wings. Sexes are alike.

Distribution: Eastern Panama in Central America south across the Amazon Basin to Bolivia, Brazil and northern Argentina. Now very rare in Panama and also at the southern tip of its range in Argentina, where there never appears to have been an established population.
Size: 29–37in (74–94cm).
Habitat: Forested areas.
Nest: Large hollow trees, sometimes on cliff faces.
Eggs: 2, white.
Food: Fruits, seeds and nuts.

Spix macaw (Little blue macaw, *Cyanopsitta spixii*, E): 22in (56cm)
The last known survivor of this species in the wild disappeared toward the end of 2000, so the future of the species now depends on captive breeding of approximately 60 individuals surviving in collections around the world. These small macaws have only ever been sighted in northern Bahia, northeastern Brazil. Bluish plumage with a dark, grayish area of bare skin on the face. Sexes are alike.

Great green macaw (Buffon's macaw, *Ara ambigua*, E): 30–33in (77–84cm)
There are several widely separated populations throughout its wide range, which extends from eastern Honduras to western parts of Colombia. Mainly green plumage with a prominent area of red plumage above the bill. Whitish facial skin. Blue flight feathers, and a long reddish tail with a blue tip. Sexes are alike.

Illiger's macaw (Blue-winged macaw, *Ara maracana*, E): 15in (38cm)
Deforestation has led to the disappearance of these small macaws from Argentina. They occur in wooded parts of Brazil, south of the Amazon, and to the south in Paraguay. Mainly green, with white skin around the eyes and a red forehead and rump. Some red on the belly. Sexes alike.

Red-bellied macaw (*Ara manilata*): 18in (46cm)
Northern South America, including Trinidad, south to Bolivia, Peru and northeastern Brazil. Mainly green, with a bluer head and flight feathers. Bare yellowish area of skin surrounding the eyes. Reddish belly. Sexes are alike.

Red and gold macaw

Scarlet macaw *Ara macao*

(E: Central America)

There are two different populations, with birds of Central American origin being recognizable by the blue tips to the prominent yellow feathers on the wings. Red and gold macaws are sometimes encountered in certain areas with other related multicolored macaws, such as red and green macaws, although they do not appear to hybridize in the wild. Such mixed groups are most commonly observed congregating to feed on the soil of mineral-rich cliffs in parts of Peru. The mud that the parrots consume here is believed to neutralize plant toxins that they absorb as part of their diet. It appears that, certainly within some parts of their distribution, these macaws move seasonally in search of more plentiful feeding opportunities. They eat a considerable variety of foods, feeding in trees, rather than on or near the ground, which enables them to range widely across Central and South America.

Identification: The plumage of these large macaws is scarlet-red rather than crimson, which helps to distinguish them from the red and green macaw. Bright yellow plumage on the wings provides a further simple means of recognition. Sexes alike.

Distribution: Southern Mexico to Panama; widely distributed across the Amazonian region to Bolivia.
Size: 31–38in (80–96$\frac{1}{2}$cm).
Habitat: Forested areas and savanna.
Nest: Hollow chamber in a tall tree.
Eggs: 2, white.
Food: Fruits, seeds and nuts.

Hyacinthine macaw

Hyacinth macaw *Anodorhynchus hyacinthinus* (E)

These vividly colored macaws are the biggest parrots in the world. They fly with slow wingbeats and are usually seen in pairs or small family groups. Young hyacinthine macaws are unlikely to breed until they are seven years or even older, but these are potentially long-lived birds, with a life expectancy that can be measured in decades. They face relatively few predators, although in spite of their size and very powerful bills, they can fall victim to harpy eagles. In some areas hyacinthine macaws can be seen flying after dark, when the moon is shining. They are often noisy by nature, uttering a wide range of calls.

Identification: Predominantly a distinctive, deep shade of glossy blue, with prominent areas of bare yellow skin encircling the eyes and also present on the sides of the lower bill. Sexes are alike.

Distribution: Northeastern Brazil, extending south-westward to parts of Bolivia and Paraguay.
Size: 35–39in (89–99cm).
Habitat: Areas where Mauritia and other palms are growing.
Nest: Either a hollow tree or among rocks on inaccessible cliff faces.
Eggs: 2, white.
Food: Palm nuts, fruits and even water snails.

CONURES

Conures are a group of parakeets whose distribution is confined to parts of Central and South America. Their unusual name comes from the old generic name Conurus. *They are quite social birds by nature and are often seen in noisy flocks, congregating in large numbers where food is plentiful, and even invading agricultural regions on occasion.*

Queen of Bavaria's conure

Golden conure *Guaruba guarouba* (E)

Ranking among the most colorful of all conures, this species is most commonly seen in small groups. It occurs in regions where the forest is not subject to seasonal flooding, and so is absent from areas immediately adjacent to the Amazon River. Females sometimes share the same nest hole, with chicks of widely different ages being reared inside. The nesting chamber can be surprisingly deep, extending down for at least 6½ft (2m). Deforestation is having an adverse effect on the numbers of these beautiful parrots, since they are dependent on older, more mature trees for nesting sites. Small flocks will sometimes descend to feed in fields, taking crops such as ripening maize, but they more commonly eat a variety of rainforest fruits and flowers.

Distribution: Centred on the Amazonia region of Brazil, south of the Amazon, and may range further afield.
Size: 14in (36cm).
Habitat: Rainforest extending to the edge of cultivated areas.
Nest: Cavity within a tree, up to 100ft (30m) above the ground.
Eggs: 2–4, white.
Food: Fruit and seeds, occasionally making raids on maize fields.

Identification: Heavy bill, bright yellow coloration with no orange hues. Sexes alike. Young are a darker coloration, with green streaks on their upperparts.

Sun conure

Aratinga solstitalis

The fiery coloration of these conures explains their common name. They are very social by nature, but in spite of their bright plumage, they can be hard to spot when roosting quietly on branches. When in flight, however, their sharp, harsh calls are often heard, drawing attention to the flock as it passes overhead. The coloration of sun conures often differs slightly between individuals, with some being of a brighter shade than others. The pattern of coloration is quite variable too, so it is often possible to distinguish between individuals in a flock. Large numbers of these conures may feed together on trees, and they have also been observed eating the fruits of cacti on the ground. It is possible that they move through their range according to the season, splitting up into smaller groups for much of the year.

Distribution: Occurs in northeastern parts of South America, being found mainly in parts of Guyana, Surinam and northern areas of Brazil. May also occur in French Guiana to the east.
Size: 12in (30cm).
Habitat: Palm groves, savanna and dry forest.
Nest: In hollows in palms or other trees.
Eggs: 3–4, white.
Food: Berries, other fruits, seeds and similar items. Sometimes cacti fruits.

Identification: The orange hues on the yellow plumage, black bill and smaller size distinguish this conure from Queen of Bavaria's conure. Sexes are alike. Young are much duller, being largely green.

Blue-crowned conure (*Aratinga acuticaudata*): 14in (36cm)
Occurs in separate populations in northeast, east and central-southern parts of South America. Green with dull bluish coloration on the crown. Sexes are alike.

Yellow-eared conure (*Ognorhynchus icterotis*, E): 16in (41cm)
Northern Andean region of Ecuador and Colombia. A relatively large, almost macaw-like conure. Green body, with yellow extending from the bill to the tops of the eyes and across the underside of the cheeks. Sexes are alike.

Patagonian conure (*Cyanoliseus patagonus*): up to 20in (51cm)
Southern South America. Another relatively macaw-like conure, with distinctive, brownish wings, a gray chest broken by a band of variable white feathering, and golden-yellow underparts. Orangish-red area between the legs. Nests colonially in cliff faces. Sexes are alike.

Slender-billed conure (*Enicognathus leptorhynchus*): 16in (41cm)
Restricted to Chile. Predominantly green, with red areas extending from the bill to the eyes and also present on the belly. Elongated upper mandible used to dig up roots. Also eats seeds. Sexes are alike.

Green conure (*Aratinga holochlora*): 13in (33cm)
Extends from the far south of Texas in the USA south through Central America, occurring in eastern and southern Mexico south to northern Nicaragua. Predominantly green with a prominent white eye ring of bare skin and a pale bill. May be traces of yellow on the edge of the wings. The southern subspecies, known as the red-throated conure (*A. h. rubritorquis*), is easily distinguishable by its reddish throat.

Red-fronted conure

Wagler's conure *Aratinga wagleri*

Most conures of the genus *Aratinga* are predominantly green in color, with the brighter coloration on their heads serving to distinguish the individual species. Red-fronted conures are noisy by nature, and their call notes resemble the braying of a donkey. They often congregate in large flocks consisting of as many as 300 individuals. Cliffs are favored both as roosting and breeding sites, and are an important factor in determining the precise distribution of these conures within their range.

Flocks of red-fronted conures sometimes descend into agricultural areas, where they are capable of causing serious damage to cultivated crops.

Distribution: Discontinuous distribution down the western side of South America in the Andes mountains, from Venezuela to Peru.
Size: 14in (36cm).
Habitat: Most often in forested areas with cliffs nearby.
Nest: Often located on cliff faces.
Eggs: 3–4, white.
Food: A variety of wild and cultivated seeds and fruits, including maize crops.

Identification: Red plumage may extend over the top of the head to just behind the eyes, depending on the race. Scattered red feathering may also be present on the throat. Thighs are red. Sexes alike. Young birds have greatly reduced area of red on the head.

El Oro conure

Pyrrhura orcesi

The *Pyrrhura* conures are sometimes known as the scaly-breasted conures because of the characteristic barring across their chests. Most of the species have restricted areas of distribution, and the El Oro conure was not discovered until 1980. It is believed to have a very restricted range, which may be no more than 60 miles (100km) long and 6 miles (10km) wide. There has been relatively little deforestation in this area, and the population appears to be quite stable where the forest is undisturbed. These conures are most likely to be observed feeding in the forest canopy, or flying overhead calling. They are often seen in groups of between four and 12 individuals.

Identification: Red on the crown and bend of the wing. Chest barring is relatively indistinct in this particular species. Pale bill. Sexes alike. Young birds display less red.

Distribution: Apparently centred on El Oro province, Ecuador.
Size: 9in (23cm).
Habitat: Cloud forest, at altitudes between 2,000 and 4,260ft (600–1,300m).
Nest: Probably tree hollows.
Eggs: Not recorded.
Food: Fruits and seeds.

AMAZONS AND OTHER PARROTS

Amazon parrots are widely distributed in America, from the extreme south of the USA and Mexico, south through Central America and the Caribbean to South America. They are sometimes described as green parrots because this color predominates in the plumage of many species. Pionus parrots are smaller in size, while the bizarre hawk-head is the only member of its group.

Imperial Amazon

Dominican Amazon *Amazona imperialis* (E)

The largest of all 27 species of Amazons, these parrots are also unusually colored because most Amazons are predominantly green. It is sometimes seen in the company of the red-necked Amazon, and both are most likely to be seen in the vicinity of Dominica's highest mountain, Morne Diablotin. Hurricanes and agricultural development pose serious threats to the survival of these Amazons. Imperial Amazons have a wide range of call notes, which are often loud. Their alarm call has been likened to the sound of a trumpet. Pairs nest in hollow trees, but research suggests that they may breed only every two years or so, rather than annually, and then produce only a single chick.

Distribution: The Caribbean island of Dominica in the Lesser Antilles.
Size: 18in (46cm).
Habitat: Mountainous forest.
Nest: Tree cavities.
Eggs: 2, white.
Food: Fruits, nuts, seeds and palm shoots.

Identification: Green back. Purple neck and underparts. They can be confused with birds of prey, owing to their large size and flight pattern (wingbeats followed by gliding). Sexes are alike. Young have green on the cheeks.

Black-billed Amazon

Amazona agilis

Distribution: Central and eastern parts of Jamaica.
Size: 10in (25cm).
Habitat: Wet limestone forests and agricultural areas.
Nest: Tree cavities at least 59ft (18m) off the ground.
Eggs: 2, white.
Food: Fruits, seeds and nuts.

Two distinctive species of Amazon parrot inhabit the Caribbean island of Jamaica and sometimes associate together in mixed flocks. As its name suggests, the black-billed can be easily distinguished from the yellow-billed (*A. collaria*) by its beak coloration. Breeding occurs between March and May. These Amazons are shy birds by nature, and rarely tolerate a close approach. Their green plumage helps to conceal them in forests, making them very hard to spot, especially because they will remain silent if disturbed. Sadly, deforestation in various parts of the island is thought to be having an adverse effect on their numbers.

Identification: Mainly dark green with a bluish hue on the top of the head, black ear coverts and black edging to the feathers on the back of the head. Black bill. Sexes alike, although hens may have some green feathers on the edge of the wings. Young birds lack any trace of red feathering on the wing edges, and this area is entirely green.

Mealy Amazon (*Amazona farinosa*):
15in (38cm)
Range extends from Central America,
home of the distinctive blue-crowned
race (*A. f. guatemalae*), across much of
northern South America to Brazil. A
large, green Amazon with a particularly
raucous call. Sexes are alike.

Red-necked Amazon (*Amazona
arausiaca*, E): 16in (41cm)
Restricted to the Caribbean island of
Dominica. Distinguished from the
Imperial Amazon by its predominantly
green coloration and distinctive red
area of plumage across the throat,
often extending to the upper breast.
Sexes are alike.

Thick-billed parrot (*Rhynchopsitta
pachyrhyncha*, E): 15in (38cm)
Used to range regularly from Mexico
into the US states of New Mexico and
Arizona, particularly to the Chiricahua
Mountains, but has suffered greatly from
the clearance of pine trees, the cones of
which provide its major source of food.
Mainly green, with scarlet areas on the
head, wings and thighs. Powerful bill.
Sexes are alike.

Dusky pionus (*Pionus fuscus*):
9½in (24cm)
Occurs in lowland forests from the
Colombian–Venezuelan border east to
northeastern Brazil. Unusual pinkish,
purple and bluish-brown tones in its
plumage. Sexes are alike.

Hawk-headed parrot

Red-fan parrot *Deroptyus accipitrinus*

Completely unique among parrots, the hawk-
headed possesses a stunning ruff of blue-edged,
claret-red feathers at the back of its neck, which it
can raise like a fan as part of its display. These
parrots may be seen in small groups outside the
breeding season. They feed largely in the treetops
rather than descending to the ground, and raise
their young either in natural tree hollows or in old
woodpecker nests. Hawk-heads are noisy parrots,
possessing a wide array of call notes.
They often call loudly and
fan the ruff of feathers
around the neck if alarmed.

Distribution: Northern South
America, to the east of the
Andes mountains.
Size: 12in (31cm).
Habitat: Lowland rainforest.
Nest: Tree hollows,
sometimes occupying old
woodpecker nests.
Eggs: 2–3, white.
Food: Fruit, seeds, nuts
and leaves.

Identification: These parrots
fly quite slowly, with their tail
feathers spread slightly apart.
They may be confused with
small hawks, thanks to the
rounded tips to the wings
and tail. Green back,
wings and tail. Sexes
alike. Young have
some green feathering
on the crown.

Blue-headed pionus

Blue-hooded parrot *Pionus menstruus*

The most widely distributed of the seven members of the *Pionus*
genus, and one of the commonest American
parrots, the blue-headed is often seen either
singly or in pairs, rather than in flocks.
They do congregate in larger numbers in
certain mineral-rich areas, consuming the
soil in the company of other parrots. The
mineral-rich soil is thought to neutralize toxins
absorbed from their food, which is usually
gathered in the forest canopy, although they
occasionally raid maize fields. Blue-headed pionus
are sometimes observed flying quite high and fast in a
loose formation, when they become more conspicuous than
many parrots. They often call loudly when in flight.

Identification: Rich dark blue head with black ear coverts.
Otherwise green plumage overall. Bill has reddish markings on the
sides. Sexes alike. Young birds have mainly green heads.

Distribution: Two separate
populations: from southern
Costa Rica to northern South
America; also present over a
wide area of central South
America east of the Andes.
Size: 11in (28cm).
Habitat: Lowland tropical
forest, into agricultural areas.
Nest: Tree cavities, or nest
sites created by other birds.
Eggs: 2–4, white.
Food: Seeds, fruit and nuts,
and sometimes maize.

SMALLER PARROTS AND PARAKEETS

The parrots of South America display their greatest range in size, from large macaws down to the small parrotlets that are often not much larger than the width of a human hand. Small species are often the hardest to spot, especially in a rainforest setting, because their coloration as well as their size helps to conceal their presence in this habitat.

Vulturine parrot

Pionopsitta vulturina

One of the most unusual of all parrots in terms of appearance, the vulturine parrot is so called because of its essentially unfeathered head, which is covered with fine, bristle-like plumage. It has been suggested that this characteristic has developed to stop the feathering becoming matted by fruit juices when these parrots feed. Young birds, distinguishable by their fully feathered heads, are believed to congregate in flocks on their own until they pair off for breeding. The call of the vulturine parrot is also very different from that of other parrots, and has a watery tone. These parrots are found in areas of lowland forest, where their presence is easily overlooked since they are quiet by nature.

Identification: Bald, blackish face with adjacent yellow area of plumage around the neck. Sexes alike. Young birds have fully feathered greenish heads and less yellow on the neck. Like that of the adults, the base of the bill (cere) is unfeathered and prominent.

Distribution: South of the Amazon River in north-eastern Brazil, extending in the east to the coastal zone of Brazil.
Size: 9in (23cm).
Habitat: Lowland tropical rainforest.
Nest: Unrecorded—probably in tree hollows.
Eggs: Unrecorded.
Food: Berries, other fruit and seeds gathered in the forest canopy.

White-bellied caique

Pionites leucogaster

Most likely to be seen in small flocks, white-bellied caiques are quite bold by nature, and often tolerate a relatively close approach before flying off rapidly. Their wings make an unusual whirring sound as they become airborne, and are quite small relative to the birds' size. If disturbed, white-bellied caiques call out loudly. Their other call notes are more varied, and some have been likened to the sounds of tapirs. They sometimes associate in groups with blue-headed pionus, and can often be observed close to waterways, being less common in drier parts of their range in the south. Three distinct races of the white-bellied caique are recognized through the range of this species. In some cases the coloration of the tail feathers is yellow rather than green, and the plumage on the thighs is also yellow.

Identification: White underparts and a yellow head distinguish this caique from other parrots in the region, notably the black-headed caique, which borders its northerly range. Sexes alike. Young birds have a brown crown and nape.

Distribution: Occurs in the area of central South America, south of the Amazon from Brazil to south-eastern Peru and northern Bolivia. Has also been reported in the eastern part of Ecuador, but its occurrence here is still to be verified.
Size: 9in (23cm).
Habitat: Lowland rainforest.
Nest: Usually high up in a tree cavity.
Eggs: 2–4, white.
Food: Berries, other fruit, seeds and nuts.

Red-winged parrotlet

Blue-fronted parrotlet *Touit dilectissima*

Distribution: Panama south into northwestern South America where the species' precise range is still unclear. Extends south to near the Peruvian border.
Size: 6in (15cm).
Habitat: Wet forests, sometimes ranging up into cloud-forest areas.
Nest: Chamber located in arboreal termites' nests.
Eggs: Probably about 5, white.
Food: Berries, other fruit, blossoms and seeds.

The parrotlets can all be recognized by their small size and rather dumpy body shape, with short, squat tails. The red-winged, like related parrotlets, is quiet and easily overlooked in the forest canopy. Although three separate populations of these inconspicuous parrotlets have been identified, it is possible that these are not actually isolated, although this species is considered to be scarce in Central America. Red-winged parrotlets feed and roost in small groups, eating both seeds and fruit. They fly low over the trees, when their high-pitched calls are most likely to be heard. Their yellow underwing coverts are also conspicuous in flight.

Identification: Mainly green, with blue feathering on the front of the head. Pronounced areas of red feathering on the sides of the wings, reduced in hens. Young birds resemble hens, but their heads are predominantly green.

Spot-winged parrotlet (*Touit stictoptera*): 7in (18cm)
Scattered distribution in the eastern Andes, from Colombia to Peru, in mature, subtropical forests. Mainly green with blackish-brown area on the wings. Sexes are similar except that cocks have white, spot-like edging to some of the wing feathers.

Golden-plumed conure (*Leptosittaca branickii*, E): 14in (35^1/$_2$cm)
Andean region in forested areas. Recognizable by elongated, tufted band of yellow plumage under the eyes; rest of the plumage is green. Orangish suffusion on the breast. Sexes alike.

Rusty-faced parrot (*Hapalopsittaca amazonina*): 9in (23cm)
Occurs at relatively high altitudes in the Andean cloud forests of Colombia and Venezuela. Mainly green, with yellow streaking on the sides of the heads, lacking in young birds. Sexes alike.

Short-tailed parrot (*Graydidascalus brachyurus*): 9in (23cm)
Widely distributed along the Amazon and its tributaries, from Peru, Ecuador and Colombia in the west to French Guiana and Brazil. Predominantly green parrots with a plump appearance. Very noisy by nature. Often seen in large numbers on river islands. Sexes alike.

Cobalt-winged parakeet

Blue-winged parakeet *Brotogeris cyanoptera*

Distribution: Western area of the Amazon Basin, from Venezuela to Bolivia.
Size: 7in (18cm).
Habitat: Forests and open areas where trees are available nearby for roosting.
Nest: Probably tree holes but may use arboreal termite mounds.
Eggs: 5, white.
Food: Fruit and seeds.

Identification: Predominantly green, with cobalt-blue flight feathers and an orange spot under the chin. Sexes alike. Young birds have grayer bills.

The seven species of the *Brotogeris* group are represented in both Central and South America. They are quite dumpy birds, all of similar size, with relatively narrow tail feathers. Green usually predominates in their plumage. They tend to be noisy, social birds by nature. Cobalt-winged parakeets are fast on the wing. Although they are sometimes seen flying across open areas and clearings, they tend to spend more time in the forest canopy than other members of the group, where their size and coloration make them relatively hard to observe. They are most likely to be encountered in lowland forests, sometimes in areas where seasonal flooding occurs.

WOODPECKERS

These birds are highly adapted to living in woodlands, and are able to hop up vertical trunks supported by their rigid, prong-like tail feathers and their powerful feet and claws. The largest member of the family, the ivory-billed woodpecker (Campephilus principalis), which measures 20in (50cm), is now believed to be extinct in the southeastern USA, with just a tiny population surviving on Cuba.

Cream-colored woodpecker

Celeus flavus

Distribution: Colombia, Guyana, Surinam and French Guiana south to Bolivia and Brazil.
Size: 11in (28cm).
Habitat: Wooded areas near water, ranging from mangrove to rainforest.
Nest: Tree hollow.
Eggs: 3, white.
Food: Invertebrates and possibly some vegetable matter.

In spite of their name, some of these woodpeckers are of a more yellowish shade than others, while buffish and cinnamon-white individuals are also known. Cream-colored woodpeckers have a very distinctive call that sounds somewhat like a laugh. There is usually a close bond between members of a pair. These woodpeckers are likely to be encountered in a wide range of habitats, from mangrove swamps to savanna. They can also be found in agricultural areas, particularly coffee plantations, where they help to control insect pests.

Identification: Predominantly cream, although coloration can be quite variable, with an obvious crest. Crimson patches on the sides of the face. Wing coverts are brownish. Tail is black. Odd brown feathers may be apparent on the underparts. Hens lack the crimson plumage on the sides of the head.

Crimson-bellied woodpecker

Campephilus haematogaster

These large woodpeckers are not easy to spot, especially since they are more likely to be observed as individuals rather than as pairs or in larger groups. They are most commonly seen in the understorey, frequently quite low down on bigger trees in dense forest. They eat a variety of invertebrates, including the larvae of wood-boring beetles up to 6in (15cm) long, which they pull out from the bark using their strong, chisel-shaped bills. Crimson-bellied woodpeckers make a double rap when drumming, like related species, and have an alarm call that resembles a loud squeal. They tend to frequent relatively wet areas of montane habitat. The plumage of these woodpeckers typically appears less brightly colored when it is worn, and the white barring on the undersides of the flight feathers can be seen only in flight.

Identification: Prominent area of red on the head. Two black stripes beneath, bordered by two yellowish-white stripes. The lower one is more extensive in hens, whose black feathering extends to the lower neck. Wings are black, rump is crimson. Underparts are crimson and black, and are blacker in the case of hens.

Distribution: Western Panama south to parts of Ecuador. Occurs in two apparently separate populations, with the nominate race ranging from eastern parts of Colombia south to Peru.
Size: 13in (33cm).
Habitat: Tropical forest.
Nest: Tree hollow.
Eggs: 2, white.
Food: Invertebrates.

Red-bellied woodpecker (*Melanerpes carolinus*): 9in (23cm)
Southeastern Canada, and USA to southern Florida and the Gulf Coast. Red plumage from the bill over the head to the nape of the neck. This characteristic is usually absent in hens, or very greatly reduced. Black-and-white barred back and wings. Underparts are pinkish gray. These woodpeckers eat a wide variety of foods, ranging from fish to oranges, through the year.

Acorn woodpecker (*Melanerpes formicivorus*): 9in (23cm)
Western USA through Central America to Colombia. Black area encircling front of the face with a white band behind, encircling the eyes. Black streaking on the white breast, and the rest of the underparts are white. Scarlet area on the nape is absent in hens. Most likely to be found in oak woodland. Stores acorns as winter food.

Golden-naped woodpecker (*Melanerpes chrysauchen*): 7½in (19cm)
Costa Rica to Panama and northern Colombia. Distinctive golden-yellow nape and red crown, with black plumage extending from the sides of the head to the back, where there is a broad white stripe. Hens are less colorful overall. Often drums on wood with its bill.

Powerful woodpecker (*Campephilus pollens*): 14½in (37cm)
Andean region, from Colombia to Peru. Scarlet crest with white stripes extending from each side of the face over the wings, to create a V-shape here. White back and rump. Underparts barred. Hens lack the scarlet on the head, and have darker underparts.

Black-backed three-toed woodpecker

Picoides arcticus

Ranging over a huge area, these woodpeckers are most likely to be seen where there are numerous dead pine trees, especially if the surrounding area is flooded. They often occur in groups, breeding together in close proximity where conditions are favorable. In some years, flocks may move further south than usual, occasionally crossing into the US states of Nebraska, New Jersey and Ohio. This type of movement, known as an irruption, is usually the result of a shortage of food.

Distribution: Canada and northern USA, from Alaska east to Newfoundland in the north, and south to New York state and California.
Size: 9½in (24cm).
Habitat: Coniferous forest.
Nest: Tree hollow.
Eggs: 2–6, white.
Food: Mainly invertebrates, but also some vegetable matter, such as nuts.

Identification: Yellowish plumage on the head and crown, with two white stripes on each side of the face separated by an irregular, broad, black band. Wings and back are blackish, with some whitish feathering. The flanks of some birds are blacker than others, depending on the subspecies. The short inner hind toe, equivalent to the thumb, is missing, helping these birds to climb vertically. Hens are smaller and lack any yellow on the crown. Young birds are browner in color, but with more white plumage on the wings. Markings on the underparts are not as clear as those of adults.

Red-headed woodpecker

Melanerpes erythrocephalus

These woodpeckers eat a wide range of plant and animal foods, and their diet is influenced by the season. They are unusual in that they hunt not only by clambering over the bark of trees, but also by hawking insects in flight. They will even swoop down onto the ground and hop along there seeking prey. Red-headed woodpeckers also raid the nests of other birds, seizing both eggs and chicks, as well as catching mice. In northern parts of their range, these woodpeckers often migrate southward during the colder months of the year, seeking plentiful supplies of acorns and beech nuts when other foods are in short supply. They also lay down stores of food, concealing larger insects in cavities or hiding them under the bark, and returning to eat them later.

Distribution: Canada and the USA, ranging from Manitoba and southern Ontario in the north, southward to Florida.
Size: 9½in (24cm).
Habitat: Open woodland.
Nest: Tree hollow.
Eggs: 4–10, white.
Food: Plant and animal matter.

Identification: Scarlet plumage covering the head, bordered by a narrow band of black feathering. White underparts, bluish-black coloration on the back, part of the wings and the tail. Sexes are alike. Young birds are much browner overall, including the head.

TANAGERS

The tanager group is comprised of approximately 240 different species, with representatives found throughout America. The largest of the tanagers, up to 11in (28cm) long, is the magpie tanager (Cissopis leveriana), so-called because of its black and white plumage. Tanagers occur at a wide range of altitudes, from sea level up into the Andean region. Some North American species are migratory.

Paradise tanager

Tangara chilensis

These tanagers are rather shy by nature, and their coloration makes them hard to recognize against a dark woodland background. They are lively, restless birds with alert, curious natures. They occur in loose flocks, typically comprised of 10–15 individuals, and are sometimes seen in the company of related species. Paradise tanagers usually seek out food in the upper part of the canopy, hopping along the branches there and grabbing spiders and other invertebrates as well as seeking berries and fruit.

Left: A paradise tanager on its nest. The Yuracares Native American tribe calls these birds "yeri yeri" because of the sound of their calls.

Identification: Essentially green on the sides of the face, violet-blue throat with vibrant sky-blue underparts. Rump red, with the back of the head and wings black. Sexes alike. There is some subspecific variation, and the rump color is paler in immature birds.

Distribution: Colombia east to French Guiana and Brazil. Also present in Peru and Ecuador. Although their scientific name suggests otherwise, these tanagers are not found as far south as Chile, reaching only as far as northern Bolivia.
Size: 5in (12¹/₂cm).
Habitat: Lowland areas of woodland and forest.
Nest: Cup-shaped, made of vegetation.
Eggs: 2, whitish with purple-red speckling.
Food: Fruit and invertebrates.

Beryl-spangled tanager

Tangara nigroviridis

Social by nature, beryl-spangled tanagers are usually observed either in pairs or small flocks comprised of up to 15 individuals. They move fast, rarely resting for any time on a perch. These tanagers remain relatively close to the ground when foraging. They adopt a distinctive posture with their head down when seeking spiders and similar creatures, peering under branches and leaves. Their necks are surprisingly flexible, allowing these tanagers to pluck invertebrates from relatively inaccessible sites. There is some variation between races in their bluish-green plumage.

Identification: Black plumage around the bill, extending in a band around the eyes and over the back, is separated by bluish-green plumage, which is also present on the crown. Violet hues apparent over the wings. The rump is greenish blue, while the underparts are blackish with pronounced blue spangling. Sexes alike.

Distribution: Colombia and Venezuela south to parts of Ecuador, Peru and Bolivia.
Size: 5in (12¹/₂cm).
Habitat: Relatively open areas of forest.
Nest: Cup-shaped, made of vegetation.
Eggs: 2, creamy white to pale green, with darker speckling.
Food: Berries, other fruit and invertebrates.

Blue-winged mountain tanager

Anisognathus flavinucha

These relatively large tanagers are the most common member of their genus in Colombia. They tend to be encountered throughout their range at lower levels than other related species, usually frequenting altitudes of 4,600–8,500ft (1,400–2,600m). They are most likely to be observed toward the tree-tops, in groups comprised of up to ten individuals. Blue-winged mountain tanagers are quiet by nature; their trilling calls are unlikely to betray their presence from any distance away. Their gape enables them to swallow some berries whole, while on other occasions they pull the skin off first.

Identification: Yellow stripe running over the crown, bordering black areas of plumage on the head. Underparts a matching shade of rich yellow. Back olive-yellow, with blue shoulder patches apparent on the wings. Color of tail and rump varies, depending on subspecies. Sexes are alike.

Distribution: Colombia and Venezuela south into Bolivia.
Size: 7½in (19cm).
Habitat: Forested areas in the Andean region.
Nest: Cup-shaped, made of vegetation.
Eggs: 2, greenish-white, speckled.
Food: Berries, other fruit and invertebrates.

Green and gold tanager (*Tangara schrankii*): 4½in (12cm)
Colombia and Venezuela to Ecuador, Peru, Bolivia and Brazil. Green plumage on the sides of the body and tail. The crown, underparts and rump are golden yellow. Forehead and area surrounding the eyes black. Hens and young birds have a green rump and black spotting on the crown.

Bay-headed tanager (*Tangara gyrola*): 4½in (12cm)
Costa Rica via Panama to Colombia, to French Guiana, Brazil, Ecuador, Peru and Bolivia. Quite variable in coloration through its wide range, but generally brown plumage on the head. Wings greenish, while underparts may vary from green to blue.

Crested ant tanager (*Habia cristata*, E): 7½in (19cm)
Confined to the western Andes of Colombia. Long, narrow, scarlet crest feathers, with scarlet throat. Upperparts reddish, with brown wings, underparts grayish. Young birds predominantly brown and have no crest. Feeds mainly on various insects, swooping down to snatch army ants on the march.

Grass-green tanager (*Chlorornis riefferii*): 8in (20cm)
Distribution extends through the Andean region, from Colombia via Peru to Bolivia. Brilliant grass-green coloration offset against chestnut-brown plumage on the sides of the face, and in the vent region. Bill and legs are red in adults. Bills of immatures are brown.

Purple honeycreeper

Cyanerpes caeruleus

Honeycreepers often move extensively through their range, with their local distribution being affected by the whereabouts of flowering trees. Their narrow, curving bills enable these birds to probe flowers to obtain nectar, but their bill shape also allows them to feed on seed pots and to seize small invertebrates. Purple honeycreepers are sufficiently agile to catch insects in flight, although they cannot hover in front of flowers as hummingbirds do. They will, however, dive down to seize spiders that try to escape off branches by dropping down on gossamer threads.

Identification: A rich shade of purple, with a black bib under the throat and black on the wings. Legs are yellow. Hens are green, with yellowish striations on the underparts. Sky-blue patches extending back from the corners of the bill and on the top of the head.

Distribution: Panama south-east via Colombia to French Guiana, and south to Ecuador, Peru, Bolivia and Brazil.
Size: 4in (10cm).
Habitat: Flowering trees.
Nest: Cup-shaped nest made of vegetation.
Eggs: 2, white with reddish-chocolate blotches.
Food: Nectar, berries, other fruit and invertebrates.

BLACKBIRDS
AND HUMMINGBIRDS

*The bills of both these diverse groups of birds are very significant in terms of their lifestyles.
The American blackbirds (quite unrelated to the European blackbird) use their bill rather like a
knitting needle to weave intricate nests; the shape of the hummingbird's bill has a decided impact
on the type of flowers on which it feeds.*

Crested oropendola

Psarocolius decumanus

During the breeding season, the remarkable call of
the male crested oropendola is heard frequently.
It has been likened to the noise made by a
finger repeatedly plucking the teeth of
a plastic comb. These oropendolas live
in colonies comprised of several cock
birds, one of whom is dominant,
and as many as 30 hens. The
crest is used as part of the
male's display, which consists
of elaborate posturing as well
as distinctive singing.
Ordinary call notes are
much shorter and
harsher in tone, and are
uttered by both sexes.
When foraging
for food, crested
oropendolas
frequently
associate with blue
jays (*Cyanocorax* species).

Identification: Mainly
black, with striking blue
eyes and a slight crest. Large,
relatively straight, pointed white
bill, which is characteristic.
Chestnut-brown rump, with
yellow in the tail feathers and
brown undertail coverts. Hens are
similar but duller, and lack a crest.

Distribution: Western
Panama south via Colombia
to northern Argentina and
southeastern Brazil.
Size: 17in (43cm) cock; hen
typically 13in (33cm).
Habitat: Typically lowland
wooded areas.
Nest: Suspended nest built
off tree branches.
Eggs: 1–2, pale green
or grayish.
Food: Mainly invertebrates.

*Left: The entrance to the nest of
the crested oropendola is at the
top, and isolated trees are
favored for nesting.*

Troupial

Icterus icterus

These attractive icterids
(blackbirds) are the national bird of
Venezuela, and have been introduced to
islands in the Caribbean, notably Bonaire,
although they also occur naturally on the
Netherlands Antilles. It can be difficult to
distinguish young birds from the adults on the basis
of their plumage, but the bare area of skin
surrounding the eyes is a duller shade of blue with
a grayish hue in immature specimens (as pictured). Unlike
other icterids, troupials do not build their own nests.
Instead, they take over those built by other birds,
particularly rufous-fronted thornbirds (*Phacellodomus
rufifrons*) and sometimes great kiskadees (*Pitangus
sulphuratus*). Troupials then modify the nests with a new
lining to meet their own needs.

Identification: Black head and
bill, with black on the back
and on the wings, where there is
also white plumage. The plumage
itself is quite rough in texture
here. The remainder of the body
is orangish yellow in color, with a
black tail. Bluish area of skin
surrounds the eyes. Sexes alike.

Distribution: Northern South
America from Colombia and
Venezuela to the Caribbean.
Size: 9in (23cm).
Habitat: Relatively dry
woodland.
Nest: Covered (roofed) nest.
Eggs: 3, white or pale pink
with dark blotches.
Food: Mainly frugivorous, but
also eats invertebrates, and
may rob other nests for eggs.

Gorgeted woodstar (*Acestrura heliodor*):
2½in (6.5cm)
Mountainous areas of eastern Panama south to
Venezuela and northwestern Ecuador. The
gorgeted is the smallest of the woodstars.
Stunning pinkish gorget under the throat, lacking
in hens, with white feathering on the chest.
Remainder of the plumage is mainly green. The
underparts of hens are cinnamon.

Wedge-billed hummingbird (*Schistes
geoffroyi*): 3½in (9cm)
Mountainous areas from Venezuela to Bolivia.
Bronzy-green upperparts. White stripe extends
downward from each eye, with a blackish area
beneath. Short bill with a sharp point. Gorget is
brilliant green with purple plumage. White band
across upper chest. Hen has a duller gorget or
even a white throat, depending on subspecies.

Purple-crowned fairy hummingbird (*Heliothryx
barroti*): 4in (10cm)
Southeastern Mexico south to western Ecuador.
Distinctive, shiny violet-purple plumage on the
front of the crown, with a black stripe through
the eyes. Glossy green upperparts and pure
white underparts. Long tapering tail. Hen is
slightly larger, with a green crown.

Hoary puffleg (*Haplophaedia lugens*):
3½in (9cm)
Uplands of southwest Colombia and the
neighboring area of northern Ecuador. Green
upperparts with a coppery hue on head and
rump. Grayish-black underparts. Sexes alike.

White-tipped sicklebill hummingbird

Eutoxeres aquila

The highly distinctive, curved bill of these
hummingbirds enables them to draw nectar
from *Heliconia* flowers. They frequently
grasp onto the flower with their sharp claws
as they feed. Their relatively subdued
coloration and small size makes white-
tipped sicklebills hard to observe in
woodland, especially since they are solitary
by nature. They are also shy in contrast to
many hummingbirds, but are quite common
near their main food plant. They hunt for
small invertebrates on bark. The nest of
these hummingbirds hangs down, often
suspended off a palm frond, with a "tail"
made of plant fibers beneath.

Distribution: Costa Rica
south to northwestern Peru in
the Andean region.
Size: 4½in (11.5cm).
Habitat: Lower areas of
forest and woodland.
Nest: Cup-shaped, made of
plant fibers.
Eggs: 2, white.
Food: Nectar, pollen and
small invertebrates.

Identification: Characteristic sickle-
shaped bill, with lower part
being yellow. Glossy deep-
green upperparts, and
heavy black-and-white
streaking on the
underparts. The
bronzy-green tail
feathers have broad
white tips. Sexes
are alike, but hens
have slightly shorter
wings compared
to cocks.

Long-tailed hermit

Phaethornis superciliosus

Distribution: Mexico south
to northern Bolivia and the
Amazonian region of Brazil,
although distribution is not
continuous through this area.
Size: 5in (13cm).
Habitat: Lower levels in
forest and woodland.
Nest: Cone-shaped, made of
plant fibers.
Eggs: 2, white.
Food: Nectar, pollen and
small invertebrates.

The body of these hummingbirds is tiny compared with the
length of their bill—which accounts for about a third of
their body length—and their long tail feathers. As is usual
behavior with hummingbirds, males are highly territorial,
and each establishes a small area, singing there for long
periods and driving away potential rivals. The repetitive call
note may be repeated up to 100 times each minute in an
attempt to attract any female in the vicinity. After mating,
the hen will build the nest and incubate and rear the chicks
on her own. She keeps
her head up when
incubating, but the nest is
usually concealed beneath
a palm frond or similar
leafy vegetation.

*Left: The hen of the long-tailed
hermit always incubates the eggs
facing the vegetation that
conceals the nest.*

Identification: Dull
shade of brown with
bronzy-green suffusion
over the back. Buff
edging to the rump. Grayish-buff
underparts, becoming buff on
the belly, with distinctive white
tips to the central tail feathers.
Sexes are alike.

THE TURKEY, THE HOATZIN AND CURIOUS NOCTURNAL BIRDS

America is home to one of the best-known and also some of the most bizarre birds in the world. The wild turkey is the original ancestor of all of today's domestic strains, kept by farmers around the world. Grouse, too, are represented in this region. America is also home to a number of other distinctive and highly specialized birds, such as the hoatzin, oilbird and the potoos.

Wild turkey

Meleagris gallopavo

These large members of the fowl family are difficult to spot in their natural woodland habitat because the barring on their plumage breaks up their outline very effectively to create good camouflage. Shafts of sunlight filtering through the trees highlight the natural iridescence in the plumage, with shades of green appearing on the feathering from some angles. The wild turkey is unmistakable, especially when the male erects his tail feathers into a fan-shape as part of his courting display. The color of his bare skin intensifies during the breeding season, and he often utters a loud gobbling call. Males, called stags, frequently live in the company of several females. It is only wild turkeys that have rusty brown tips to their tail feathers—those of domestic turkeys are white.

Identification: Bare head, which is predominantly bluish. Prominent red beard extending down from the throat, lacking in hens. Black barring on the wings and tail, and the body is mostly bronzy brown in color.

Distribution: Southern USA south into Mexico. It has a very patchy distribution that has given rise to numerous localized subspecies, especially in western parts of the range.
Size: 48in (122cm) cock; 36in (91½cm) hen. Birds from the north are larger than those found further south.
Habitat: Wooded areas, including swampland.
Nest: Scrape on the ground.
Eggs: 8–15, buff with dark brown spots.
Food: Berries, seeds and nuts, also invertebrates.

Oilbird

Steatornis caripensis

Distribution: Western Panama, Ecuador and Peru east to French Guiana.
Size: 19in (48cm).
Habitat: Caves and cliffs.
Nest: Made from regurgitated seed.
Eggs: 2–4, white with brown blotches.
Food: Fruit.

The oilbird is the only fruit-eating bird in the world that feeds at night. It spends its days roosting in the black interior of caves. Oilbirds have large eyes that glow red when a light is shone at them. They rely on a similar navigation system to bats, known as echolocation, to avoid collisions with objects when flying around in darkness. The system involves uttering a constant series of sharp calls while in flight, and listening to the echoes that bounce back to avoid flying into objects. Oilbirds will fly long distances—up to 16 miles (25km)—from their roosting caves in search of fruit each night.

Identification: Prominent hooked bill and very long wings. Rufous-brown upperparts with white spots edged with black running across the wings. Similar but smaller white-spotted patterning on the head and underparts, which are otherwise cinnamon-white. Long, tapering tail barred with black. Cock is grayer than the hen.

Great potoo

Nyctibius grandis

During the daytime the large eyes of the great potoo are dark, but they take on an eerie orange glow at night when these birds become active. They hunt large flying insects on the wing, swooping down to catch them. During the day giant potoos rest motionless on a tall branch in a hunched-up position, and their cryptic coloration helps to conceal their presence. They generally call only on moonlit nights, their vocalizations comprised of a series of guttural notes and louder, harsh, grating sounds. When breeding, the hen does not build a nest but simply lays her egg on a suitable area of a tree where it cannot roll away.

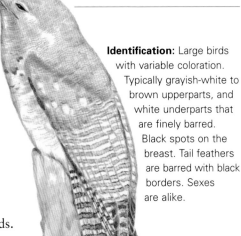

Identification: Large birds with variable coloration. Typically grayish-white to brown upperparts, and white underparts that are finely barred. Black spots on the breast. Tail feathers are barred with black borders. Sexes are alike.

Distribution: Panama south to Peru and southern Brazil.
Size: 20in (51cm).
Habitat: Gallery forest, especially at the edges.
Nest: Knotholes or similar hollows in trees.
Eggs: 1, white with darker markings.
Food: Mainly insects.

Spruce grouse (*Dendragapus canadensis*): 16in (41cm)
From Alaska south to northern parts of the neighboring USA. Prominent red area above the eye. Forehead down to the throat and upper breast are black with a white border. White barring on the flanks. Grayish upperparts. Hens are much duller, lacking the red and black areas, and are significantly smaller in size.

Ruffed grouse (*Bonasa umbellus*): 18in (46cm)
Alaska and northwestern Canada to the central USA. Distinguishable by the slight crest and ruff of black or reddish-brown feathering on the neck. There are two color phases—the reddish-brown rather than gray phase predominates in southwestern British Columbia, in Canada. Hens have a shorter ruff and incomplete tail band.

Lyre-tailed nightjar (*Uropsalis lyra*): 30in (76cm) cock; 10in (25cm) hen
In highland areas of Colombia and Venezuela to Ecuador and Peru. Very distinctive ribbon-like tail, up to three times as long as the body. Brownish black with rufous barring and spots. Hens have shorter tails that lack the white tips.

Squirrel cuckoo (*Piaya cayana*): 17in (43cm)
Ranges from northwestern Mexico south to Bolivia, Paraguay, Argentina and Uruguay, with 18 different races being recognized. Chestnut-brown head and wings, with grayish lower underparts. Long tail with pale tips to the feathers. Bare skin around the eyes is red in birds found east of the Andes mountains; greenish-yellow elsewhere. Sexes are alike.

Hoatzin

Opisthocomus hoazin

The hoatzin is often considered one of the most primitive birds on the planet, not just in terms of its appearance, but also because its chicks suggest a link back to reptile ancestors in the distant past. They hatch with claws on their wings, which enable them to grasp onto branches and climb back up if they slip off their fragile nest platform into water beneath. However, they can also swim well at this stage. The claws are lost once they are able to fly properly, although hoatzins are not powerful on the wing, preferring to glide short distances and hop from branch to branch. This is partly a reflection of their bulky, leaf-based diet, which means that their crop is voluminous in size and affects their balance.

Identification: Long neck, loose crest and long tail with buff tipping. Plumage is bronzy olive with buff streaking on the upperparts. Throat and breast feathering are very pale buff. Lower underparts are chestnut. Sexes are alike.

Distribution: Northern Amazonian region of Brazil.
Size: 25in (63.5cm).
Habitat: Trees adjoining slow-flowing stretches of water.
Nest: Loose platform of sticks.
Eggs: 2–5, pinkish cream with pink, brown or blue spots.
Food: Leaves and shoots.

BIRDS OF PREY

These aerial predators often spend much of their time on the wing, gliding over the forest, and are thus most likely to be seen from vantage points that look down over the forest canopy. Whereas eagles and falcons seek their prey during the day, the role of night-time hunter is filled by owls.

Harpy eagle

Harpia harpyja

The immense power and strength of these eagles makes them fearsome predators, able to catch creatures ranging from birds such as large macaws to monkeys, sloths and even pigs. Reptiles such as iguanas and large snakes may also fall victim to these eagles. They are believed to use not just keen eyesight but also acute hearing to detect potential quarry in the forest canopy. However, they often prefer to hunt in clearings, or at areas where animals congregate, such as water sources. In the early morning, it is sometimes possible to see these magnificent eagles perched rather than flying overhead.

Identification: The female harpy eagle is much larger than the male, potentially weighing twice at much as her partner, up to 20lb (9kg). The head is grayish with a prominent, divided black crest. Upper chest is blackish, and underparts are white, aside from black-and-white barring on the tail feathers. There is fainter barring on the thighs. Wings are blackish. Young take at least five years to acquire full adult plumage. Their head and underparts are entirely white at first, changing gradually over successive molts.

Distribution: Southern Mexico through Central America, to Colombia and northern South America, ranging as far south as northeastern Argentina, via eastern Bolivia and Brazil.
Size: Female 41in (104cm).
Habitat: Lowland tropical forest. They rarely soar over the forest, preferring instead to fly close to the canopy.
Nest: Platform of sticks.
Eggs: 2, whitish.
Food: Vertebrates.

Black and chestnut eagle

Oroaetus isidori

These eagles are most likely to be seen at altitudes of around 6,600ft (2,000m), but they have been observed from sea level up to 11,500ft (3,500m). Relatively little is known about their habits, and they are hard to observe since they hunt mainly in the canopy, preying on quite large creatures, including monkeys, which they seize in their powerful talons. Large trees are chosen to support the weight of their nest, which can measure up to 6½ft (2m) in diameter. The cock bird is responsible for feeding the single chick, and appears to concentrate on hunting squirrels for it. The young eagle spends about four months in the nest, after which time its plumage darkens over successive molts until it assumes its adult coloration at four years old.

Identification: Head, including crest feathers, back, wings and top of the thighs are black. Lower chest and underparts are chestnut streaked with black. Tail is grayish with a black band at its tip. Iris is orange-yellow. Feet are yellow. The female can be up to 8in (20cm) larger than the male.

Distribution: Northeastern Colombia and adjacent Venezuela south through Ecuador and Peru to Bolivia. Possibly no longer occurs in Argentina.
Size: Female 32in (81cm).
Habitat: Forested areas.
Nest: Platform of sticks.
Eggs: 1, whitish with brownish spots.
Food: Other vertebrates.

Sharp-shinned hawk (*Accipter striatus*):
13in (33cm)
Much of North America from Alaska and Canada south to the USA as far as Panama, with birds moving further south in winter. Also on various Caribbean islands. Slate-blue upperparts and barred tail with variable white-and-chestnut areas on the underparts. Females are larger.

Boreal owl (Tengmalm's owl, *Aegolius funereus*): 11½in (29cm)
Occurs in a broad band across North America, from Alaska south to Oregon in the west and down to New Mexico. Distribution closely linked with coniferous forest. Brown wings with white spots. Underparts are chestnut with large whiter areas. Whitish facial disk with blackish edging. A separate race occurs in northern Europe and Asia. Females are larger.

Northern goshawk (*Accipter gentilis*):
26in (66cm)
North America to Mexico. A separate population is present through northern Europe and Asia. Variable depth of coloration. Wings are grayish. Underparts are white with grayish barring that extends right up around the neck. Darker area of plumage on the head and behind the eyes. Hens are larger.

Plumbeous forest falcon (*Micrastur plumbeus*):
15in (38cm)
Southwest Colombia and northern Ecuador. Small, with dark grayish head and back. Barred underparts, with a characteristic single white band midway down the white-tipped tail feathers.

Great grey owl

Strix nebulosa

These owls move quite extensively through their large range, with North American individuals even having been sighted in the vicinity of New York on occasion. Much of this movement is triggered by the availability of food, especially voles, which these owls hunt almost exclusively during the breeding season. Pairs will often take over the abandoned nests of other birds of prey such as buzzards, although they sometimes nest on the ground. The number of eggs in the clutch is directly related to the availability of food, with breeding results therefore being closely correlated with fluctuations in vole populations.

Distribution: Circumpolar, from northern Canada and Alaska south to California, Idaho and Wyoming. A separate population extends across the far north of Europe and Asia.
Size: 27in (69cm).
Habitat: Coniferous forest.
Nest: Often a platform of sticks.
Eggs: 3–6, white.
Food: Small vertebrates, especially voles.

Identification: Plumage coloration consists mainly of gray streaking and barring on a white background. The dark markings on the so-called facial disk that surrounds the eyes form concentric rings. Yellowish bill, with a blackish patch beneath. Tail is relatively long. Hens are larger in size.

Great horned owl

Bubo virginianus

These owls are not found in areas of dense forest such as the Amazon. They prefer instead to hunt in semi-open terrain, where their keen eyesight enables them to swoop down on small mammals that form the basis of their diet. They are opportunistic hunters, however, and will take a much wider range of prey, from insects and amphibians to other birds, including smaller owls. Males are quite vocal, and sing loudly to attract a mate. Pairs split up at the end of the breeding season, but may reunite again later. They breed in a wide range of locations; an unpleasant stench may give away the location of the nest site because the male may stockpile food here for the offspring.

Identification: Variable through the species' wide range. Northerly populations generally have more brown in their plumage and on the facial disk. Populations further south have a more buff tone to the feathering. Bill is grayish black. Iris is yellow. Hens are larger than cocks.

Right: The name of these owls comes from the appearance of their so-called ear tufts.

Distribution: Alaska and Canada south over virtually the entire USA and Central America. South America, from Colombia and Ecuador through Peru to Bolivia and east to Guyana; also south to Brazil and central Argentina.
Size: 22in (56cm).
Habitat: Lightly wooded areas.
Nest: Abandoned nest or on the ground.
Eggs: 2–6, white.
Food: Small vertebrates.

GROUND BIRDS

The rhea is the largest bird found in America today. The fossil record reveals that there used to be more gigantic birds, some of which were fearsome hunters, in this region before the southern landmass was invaded by predatory mammals from further north. A variety of other ground birds, especially quail, also now occur in this part of the world.

Greater rhea

Common rhea *Rhea americana*

The size of rheas prevents them from flying, but they are well equipped to defend themselves from most predators, and are able to run at speeds in excess of 37mph (60km/h). Their wings are larger than those of other flightless birds, with a claw on each so they can inflict serious injury at close quarters. Social by nature, rheas live in loose groups. When breeding, a number of hens are attracted to the male's nest and are persuaded to lay their eggs there. The eggs are golden yellow at first, changing to a whitish tone. The cock incubates the eggs and cares for the young chicks, which all hatch within a day or so of each other and start following him.

Identification: Tall and long-necked with grayish-brown plumage. Feathering only extends down the thighs, leaving the lower leg bare. Feet have three toes. Hens are lighter in color and slightly smaller than cocks. Pure white albino individuals are surprisingly common, especially in the Argentinian race.

Below: The elasticity of the leg muscles allows these ratites to turn quickly, while running, to avoid predators.

Distribution: Central and eastern South America, from parts of Brazil to Bolivia, Argentina and Uruguay.
Size: 55in (140cm).
Habitat: Open pampas to lightly wooded areas.
Nest: A scrape on the ground.
Eggs: Typically 13–30, golden yellow, then whitish.
Food: Omnivorous.

Common bobwhite

Northern bobwhite *Colinus virginianus*

Taxonomists have recognized at least 22 different races of these quail, and color variation is quite marked in some cases. Differences in size are also apparent, with individuals found in southerly areas being smaller than those from northern regions. Common bobwhites live in groups, typically numbering around a dozen birds or so, and will invade agricultural areas, especially when crops are ripening. They generally prefer to seek cover on the ground, but will fly if threatened. Populations of these quails have also been introduced well outside their normal range, not only in other parts of the USA, including the northwest and Hawaii, but also further afield in New Zealand.

Identification: There is considerable variation through the birds' wide range. Most races have a black stripe running from the bill through the eyes, with a white stripe above and a broader white area on the throat. Chestnut underparts, usually speckled with white. Wings are brownish. Hens are duller, with buff rather than white patches on the head.

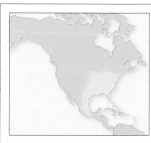

Distribution: Northeastern USA southward through Mexico into western Guatemala.
Size: 10in (25cm).
Habitat: Woodland and farmland.
Nest: Scrape in the ground lined with vegetation.
Eggs: 10–15, dull white, often with blotches.
Food: Seeds and invertebrates.

Californian quail

Callipepla californica

These quail are highly adaptable through their range, and this characteristic has also led breeding populations of these popular game birds to be established in locations as far apart as Hawaii, Chile and King Island, Australia. Nesting on the ground makes Californian quail vulnerable to predators, and although the young are able to move freely as soon as they are hatched, relatively few are likely to survive long enough to breed the following year. Overgrazing by farm animals can adversely affect their numbers, presumably because of a reduction in the available food supply, although these quail also forage in crop-growing areas, and sometimes associate in groups of up to a thousand where food is plentiful.

Distribution: Western North America, from British Columbia, in Canada, southward through California to Mexico.
Size: 11in (28cm).
Habitat: Semidesert to woodland.
Nest: Grass-lined scraping on the ground.
Eggs: About 15, creamy white with brownish splodges.
Food: Seeds, vegetation and invertebrates.

Identification: Prominent, raised black crest that slopes forward over the bill. Top of the head is chestnut, with a white band beneath and another bordering the black area of the face. Chest is grayish, flanks are speckled. Hens lack the black and white areas, with grayish faces and smaller crests.

Crested bobwhite quail (*Colinus cristatus*): 9in (23cm)
Southern Central America, from Panama to Colombia, Venezuela, French Guiana and northern Brazil. Variable appearance. Distinctive crest, usually with a white stripe near the eyes. White speckling with thin, black borders on chestnut- or buff-colored underparts. Hens are duller with a shorter crest, and lack the white eye stripe.

Scaled quail (Blue quail, *Callipepla squamata*): 11½in (29cm)
Southern USA south into Mexico. Blue-scaled plumage on the breast and neck down to the browner underparts. White-edged crest on head. Wings are brownish. Hens have a smaller crest, with brown streaking on the head and throat.

Lesser prairie chicken (*Tympanuchus pallidicinctus*): 16in (41cm)
Restricted to the states of Colorado, Kansas, Oklahoma, Texas and New Mexico in the USA. Barred brownish and white plumage, with the tail having dark banding close to the tip. Buffish-yellow plumage above the eyes, with inflatable orange-red air sacs on the sides of the head. Sexes similar, but hens lack dark tail banding.

Sharp-tailed grouse (*Tympanuchus phasianellus*): 19in (48cm)
Northern North America from Alaska across much of Canada, south into the USA, where its distribution has shrunk recently. Distinguishable from other barred members of the grouse family by its pointed tail feathers. Pinkish inflatable air sacs on the head. Underparts are speckled. Cocks are significantly larger than hens.

Rock ptarmigan

Lagopus mutus

These grouse live in a region where natural cover is very scarce, and undergo a stunning transformation in appearance through the year. Their summer plumage is mottled brown, and their winter plumage is white, enabling them to merge into the snowy landscape. When snow is on the ground, they feed on buds and twigs of shrubs such as willow, which manage to grow in this treeless region. Pairs nest in the brief Arctic summer, often choosing a site protected by shrubs. The cock stays nearby while the hen incubates alone. The chicks are covered in down when they hatch and can move easily, but are not able to fly until their flight feathers have emerged fully, at about ten days old.

Distribution: Circumpolar, extending right across the far north of North America; also present on Greenland. A similar distribution occurs in Europe and Asia.
Size: 15in (38cm).
Habitat: Tundra.
Nest: Scrape on the ground lined with vegetation.
Eggs: 6–9, creamy buff, heavily blotched and spotted with blackish brown.
Food: Buds, leaves, berries and other plant matter.

Identification: Mottled, brownish head with red above the eyes. Similar patterning across the body in summer, becoming white in winter. Blackish stripes on the face, lacking in hens.

FINCHES, BUNTINGS AND BLACKBIRDS

Many of these medium-size birds often feed on seeds for much of the year, but invertebrates become especially important in the diets of many during the breeding season. Such prey provides the essential protein that the nestlings need to grow and fledge rapidly. Most leave the nest when barely 14 days old, and the adult birds may nest again at this time.

Andean siskin

Carduelis spinescens

Distribution: The Andean region of Venezuela and Colombia to northern Ecuador.
Size: 4in (10cm).
Habitat: Scrub and relatively open countryside.
Nest: Made of plant fibers.
Eggs: 2, pale bluish white with darker markings.
Food: Seeds and invertebrates.

These siskins have a high-pitched and attractive song, often uttered in flight. They are most likely to be observed at altitudes from 5,000 to 13,500ft (1,500 to 4,100m). Here they are sometimes hard to spot in taller trees, although they also venture down to the ground in search of food. Andean siskins may be encountered in small flocks, and sometimes forage with other finches, seeking *Espletia* seeds—a particular favorite. It is not uncommon within the Ecuadorian population for some birds resembling mature cocks to actually be hens.

Identification: Black area extending from the bill to the top of the head. Plumage is greenish-yellow elsewhere and of a brighter hue on the underparts. Wings are black with distinct yellow markings across the flight feathers. Hens are duller in coloration, lacking the black cap, and with less yellow on the wings.

Hooded siskin (*Carduelis magellanica*): 5½in (14cm)
Central-southern South America, in Bolivia, Peru, Paraguay, Argentina and Uruguay. Also a northern Andean population, from Colombia to Peru, and another in southeast Venezuela, Guyana and north-west Brazil. Black head and yellowish chest and upper abdomen, becoming whiter below, with a green back. Hens are less vividly colored, with a grayish head and a greenish tone on the underparts.

Grassland sparrow (*Ammodramus humeralis*): 5in (13cm)
Colombia to French Guiana south to Bolivia, Uruguay and Argentina. Distinctive yellow plumage adjoining the bill, pronounced black streaking on the crown with chestnut edging, becoming browner on the wings. Underparts are pale brown, becoming whitish close to the vent. Sexes are alike.

Dickcissel (*Spiza americana*): 7in (18cm)
Eastern North America, overwintering in Central and northern South America. Gray head, with yellow stripe above the eye leading back from the short, conical bill. Whitish area on the throat, with black beneath. Chest is yellowish, with white lower underparts. Back and wings are brownish, with darker striations. Hens are duller in coloration, lacking the prominent black area under the throat and with gray underparts.

Saffron finch

Sicalis flaveola

Distribution: Much of South America, from Colombia to Argentina; also on Trinidad.
Size: 5½in (14cm).
Habitat: Lightly wooded areas.
Nest: Tree cavities.
Eggs: 4, pale blue with brownish spots.
Food: Seeds and invertebrates.

Although there are other finches with predominantly yellow plumage, the saffron finch is the most brightly colored member of the group, and also has one of the widest distributions. It has been introduced to localities outside its natural range, and is consequently seen in parts of Panama and Jamaica. These attractive finches can frequently be observed on the ground foraging for food, often in small groups or individual pairs. They are usually quite tame by nature, particularly in parks and urban areas.

Identification: Bright yellow underparts, becoming more orange at the front of the crown. Olive-brown wings and tail. Short, pointed bill. Hens have brown, streaked upper-parts with whitish underparts. Young birds are also streaked, with young cocks developing a yellowish neck collar and chest when they first molt into adult plumage.

Painted bunting

Passerina ciris

The cock painted bunting is popularly regarded as the most colorful of all North America's songbirds. Unfortunately, however, these relatively shy birds are not easily seen, often remaining concealed in vegetation, where their presence is more likely to be revealed by the cock's song. They have a warbling call as well as a short, harsh, warning note that is uttered at any hint of danger. The nest, too, is well hidden, and is constructed from a variety of vegetation. A pair may rear two broods in succession, and insects feature more prominently in their diet at this time. The hen builds the nest on her own and collects a variety of plant matter for this purpose, ranging from strips of bark and dead leaves to grass stems and rootlets. She chooses a well-concealed nest site, often in the fork of a tree.

Identification: Males are very colorful and unmistakable, with bluish-violet plumage on the head and rose-red throat and underparts. The wings and back are green, with darker tail and flight feathers. Hens are drab in comparison, with green upperparts, becoming more yellowish on the underside of the body, and no bars on the wing, unlike many other finches.

Distribution: Widely distributed across the southern USA and Mexico, with populations moving south in the winter as far as Panama. Also present on Cuba.
Size: 5½in (14cm).
Habitat: Lightly wooded areas and brush.
Nest: Woven nest.
Eggs: 3–5, pale blue with darker spots.
Food: Mainly seeds, some invertebrates.

Red-winged blackbird

Agelaius phoeniceus

Unrelated to the European blackbird, the red-winged blackbird is a member of the icterid family. It frequents marshland areas when nesting, but is seen in a much wider range of habitats during winter. In North America, red-winged blackbirds move southward over the winter period, typically traveling distances of about 440 miles (700km). Populations in Central American parts of their distribution tend to be sedentary throughout the year, however. There is quite marked variation in the appearance of these birds through their wide range, and it is also not uncommon for individuals to display pied markings. Both sexes sing, particularly at the start of the nesting period, and some of their call notes are different, so it is possible to tell them apart.

Identification: Only the mature male in breeding plumage displays the typical glossy black feathering and red shoulder patches with a paler buff border. Females have dark streaks running down their bodies, with more solid brownish coloration on the head, sides of the face and over the wings.

Distribution: Occurs over much of North America, breeding as far north as Alaska, and south into Central America.
Size: 9½in (24cm).
Habitat: Relatively open country.
Nest: Cup-shaped.
Eggs: 3, pale greenish-blue with dark spots.
Food: Seeds and invertebrates.

PIGEONS AND DOVES

The characteristic dumpy appearance of pigeons and doves, along with their relatively subdued coloration, means that they can be quite easily identified. There is actually no strict zoological distinction between these two groups, although the term "pigeon" is usually applied to larger species, particularly members of the Columba *genus.*

Mourning dove

Carolina dove *Zenaida macroura*

These doves are so-called because of the plaintive, mournful sound of their calls. They have benefited from the provision of bird tables, particularly in the northern part of their range, and often visit gardens for the food being offered. Their powerful wings and sleek shape help these doves to fly long distances on migration, and northerly populations overwinter in Central America. In southern US states, such as Florida, mourning doves are resident throughout the year. They prefer to seek food on the ground if not feeding on a bird table, and groups often wander across fields in search of seeds and other edible items. Mourning doves are now overwintering further north than they did in the past, partly as a result of more feeding opportunities from bird tables.

Identification: There is some variation in appearance through these doves' wide range, with cocks displaying pinkish-buff coloration on the face, extending down to the underparts, with a dark streak just above the neck. The upper surface of the wings and tail are brown, with several large dark spots evident on the wings. Hens are duller in coloration, being browner overall.

Distribution: Ranges across much of North America, from southern Canada southward across the USA through Central America to Costa Rica and Panama, but distribution is affected by the season. Also occurs on the Greater Antilles in the Caribbean.
Size: 13in (33cm).
Habitat: Lightly wooded areas.
Nest: Loose pile of twigs.
Eggs: 2, white.
Food: Seeds and some invertebrates.

Black-winged dove

Metriopelia melanoptera

The male black-winged dove has a very distinctive, rather attractive chirruping call, unlike the more usual cooing calls associated with this group of birds. His call is heard more frequently during the breeding season, as he fans his tail and flicks his wings, making the white areas of plumage on these areas more visible. These doves are often sighted in association with the smaller bare-faced ground dove (*M. ceciliae*), and frequently occur in the vicinity of puyas shrubs, which provide both roosting and breeding sites. Pairs may also nest in buildings, however, and sometimes even on the ground among rocky outcrops that provide them with some protection from possible predators. The nest itself is a relatively loose structure, and usually sited quite close to the ground.

Identification: Compact body shape. Predominantly brown, aside from the black flight feathers and tail, with a white area at the shoulder that is usually hidden. There is a slight pinkish tinge on the head, and bare orangish-red skin around the eyes. Hens are duller in color and a slightly paler shade of brown. This tends to increase in depth of color during the breeding period.

Distribution: The western side of South America, from Colombia and Ecuador through Peru, Chile and Argentina to Tierra del Fuego, at the southern tip of the continent.
Size: 9in (23cm).
Habitat: Upland arid areas.
Nest: Platform of twigs.
Eggs: 2, white.
Food: Seeds of grasses and other plants.

Inca dove (*Scardafella inca*): 8½in (22cm)
Ranges from southwestern USA south as far as
Costa Rica, up to altitudes of 9,840ft (3,000m).
Sometimes recorded as a vagrant as far north as
Ontario in Canada. Grayish olive brown, with black
scaly edging to the individual feathers over the
entire body, more bluish gray on the head, with
pinkish underparts. Underwing area seen in flight is
brown. Sexes are alike.

Buckley's ground dove (Ecuadorian ground dove,
Columbina buckleyi): 7in (18cm)
Northwestern Ecuador to northwestern Peru.
Grayish-brown upperparts and more pinkish
underparts, with grayish coloration most marked on
the head. Black underwing coverts. Hen is browner,
with less contrast in her plumage.

Eared dove (golden-necked dove, *Zenaida
auriculata*): 11in (28cm)
Occurs over most of South America, aside from the
Amazon region and the Andean uplands. Very
common, especially in northeastern Brazil, where
migratory flocks, thought to be comprised of a
million birds, can occasionally be observed. Some
variation in color through the range. Two black lines
behind and below the eyes, with a prominent green
iridescent area behind the eyes. Wings are brownish
with variable dark wing spots. Underparts are
pinkish. Hens are duller in appearance.

Spot-winged pigeon (American spotted pigeon,
Columba maculosa): 13in (33cm)
Two separate populations. One ranges from southwest Peru into western Bolivia and Argentina,
distinguishable by the white edging to the gray
feathers on the wings. The other, with more
pronounced white areas creating the impression of
spots, extends southward into southwestern Brazil,
Paraguay and Uruguay. Head and underparts have a
pinkish-gray tone. Hens grayer overall.

Gold-billed ground dove

Croaking ground dove *Columbina cruziana*

These small doves are a relatively
common sight in gardens and
parks, and have adapted well to
changes in habitat throughout
their range. They may
sometimes be seen in large
numbers where food is
abundant, seeking seeds and
other plant matter on the
ground. The distinctive
croaking calls uttered by cock
birds are more likely to be heard
during the breeding period. In common
with many other pigeons and doves, the
hen lays on a relatively flimsy nest. The
young doves may leave the nest at just
ten days old, before they are able to fly
effectively, and hide in nearby vegetation.

Identification: Predominantly brownish with
pinker underparts and grayish head. Bluish-gray
wing coverts display variably positioned reddish-
brown spots across them and a magenta stripe
across the top. The bill is yellow at the base,
while the tip is black. Hens are similar, but are
a much more even shade of
brown overall. The tail is
relatively short.

*Above: Both members of the pair
incubate the eggs.*

Distribution: Coastal region
from Ecuador through Peru to
northern Chile.
Size: 6in (15cm).
Habitat: Open woodland
and scrub.
Nest: Loose platform of
twigs.
Eggs: 2, white.
Food: Seeds of grasses and
other plants.

Bare-faced ground dove

Bare-eyed ground dove *Metriopelia ceciliae*

These doves may range at altitudes up to 15,000ft
(4,500m). When breeding, they will, unusually, seek
out holes in cliffs or even the protection offered by
buildings, rather than nesting in a tree or shrub.
In the vicinity of human habitation,
they often nest on houses, and forage
for food in surrounding gardens.
Elsewhere, they may fly quite
long distances from their
roosting sites in search of food. These
doves are very quiet by nature, and are
unlikely to betray their presence by their
calls. They are also very adept at
running along the ground to escape
from danger.

Identification: Bright area of
bare, yellowish-orange skin
encircles the eyes. Back and
wings are brownish with much
paler, buff-colored mottling
at the centers of individual
feathers. Chest is pinkish brown
with brownish
underparts.
Hens are
usually slightly
duller in coloration.

Distribution: Northern Peru
south into northern Chile,
western Bolivia and north-
west Argentina.
Size: 6in (15cm).
Habitat: Dry, upland country.
Nest: Loose platform.
Eggs: 2, white.
Food: Seeds of grasses and
other plants.

ANIS AND OTHER SMALLER HUNTERS

There are a number of smaller predatory birds that have evolved different hunting strategies. While hawks and falcons, with their high degree of aerial mobility, are well known, others such as the anis comprise a small group restricted to the Americas. They tend to feed on invertebrates, but they may also catch small vertebrates such as lizards as well.

Groove-billed ani

Crotophaga sulcirostris

These unusual members of the cuckoo clan have a relatively slim body shape and are highly social by nature, living in groups. They even sometimes associate with the slightly larger smooth-billed ani, although they can be distinguished in flight by their more languid flight pattern as they flap their wings and glide. Neither species is a powerful flier. Groove-billed anis have unusual breeding behavior: a number of females will lay eggs in the same location, reflecting their highly social natures. Up to 18 eggs have therefore been recorded in a single nest. Although these birds sometimes take over open nests abandoned by other birds, they may also construct a suitably large receptacle for their eggs from sticks and other vegetation. Groove-billed anis typically feed on the ground in groups by walking along and seizing prey that comes within reach, which may include lizards.

Identification: Dull black in color, with a distinctively shaped bill. The culmen (central ridge of the bill) is in the form of a smooth curve from the tip to the forehead. Grooves in the bill leading to the nostrils are apparent on the sides. Iris is blackish. Tail is long, with a rounded tip. Sexes similar, although hens may be slightly smaller in size.

Distribution: Southwestern USA south through Central America and Colombia, Venezuela and Guyana as far as northern Chile and Argentina; also present on Caribbean islands, from Aruba to Trinidad.
Size: 12in (30cm).
Habitat: Scrub and pastureland.
Nest: Bowl-shaped, made of vegetation.
Eggs: 4, blue-green with chalky glaze.
Food: Mainly invertebrates.

Smooth-billed ani

Crotophaga ani

This species tends to occur in more humid areas than the groove-billed ani, although it is similar in its habits. These birds are a common sight, partly as a result of their size and the way in which they frequently perch in the open, even on fences. In cattle-ranching areas in Colombia, the anis' habit of following the herd has led to them being nicknamed *garrapateros*, and they are welcomed by ranchers for removing ticks from their animals. Smooth-billed anis breed communally, like their groove-billed cousins, with as many as 29 eggs being present in a single nest.

Identification: Dull, black plumage, with a decidedly rounded shape to the tail. Bill is black, with a distinctive smooth, raised area on the top of the upper bill closest to the eyes. Sexes similar, but hens are smaller in size. Recently fledged young of this species lack the raised area on the bill, resembling groove-billed anis at this stage, although the sides of their bills are smooth.

Distribution: Southern Florida through Central America west to Ecuador and east into northern Argentina. Also present in the Caribbean.
Size: 13in (33cm).
Habitat: Brushland and open areas of country.
Nest: Large cup of vegetation.
Eggs: 4, bluish green, with chalk-like glaze.
Food: Invertebrates.

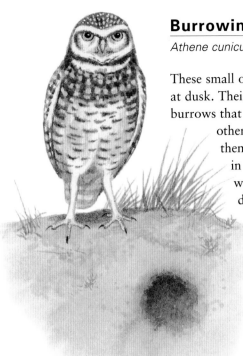

Burrowing owl

Athene cunicularia

These small owls will hunt during the day, but are most active at dusk. Their small size allows them to nest underground in burrows that may have been dug originally by prairie dogs or other rodents, or may be constructed by the birds themselves. These tunnels can extend over 10ft (3m) in length. Unusually, the owls decorate the entrance with dried cattle dung, and the odor is thought to deter potential mammalian predators from investigating inside. Burrowing owls invariably choose an open area for the entrance to their nest site, rather than concealing it in long grass.

Identification: Brownish edging on the facial disk on the sides of the eyes, with more distinctive brownish stripes beneath the yellowish bill and white eyebrows. Chest and wings are brownish, with generally whiter underparts in the case of the North and Central American race. Burrowing owls seen in Florida and the Caribbean are a darker shade of brown. Sexes alike. Young birds are buff in color, with white underparts.

Distribution: North America, from British Columbia east to Manitoba and south into Central America. Separate population in Florida and the Caribbean. Also occurs in South America, especially in the east from Brazil south to Tierra del Fuego.
Size: 10½in (27cm).
Habitat: Lightly wooded country.
Nest: Underground burrow.
Eggs: 5–6, white.
Food: Mainly larger invertebrates.

Short-eared owl (*Asio flammeus*): 17in (43cm)
Most northerly population extends across northern North America from Alaska eastward. Also present in northwest South America across the southern part of the continent and on the Galapagos Islands and Hawaii. Relatively small head, with slight tufts of plumage above the eyes. Variable coloration, brownish with white markings on the wings. Pale-streaked chest and black feathering encircling the eyes. Sexes alike.

Swainson's hawk (*Buteo swainsoni*): 22in (56cm)
From Alaska southward, mainly in the central USA. Usually migrates south for the winter to southern Brazil, Argentina and Paraguay via Central America, although some may remain in the southern USA. White area from above the bill to the throat. Chest is brown and underparts are whitish with brown barring. Head and upperparts are dark. Tail is barred. Rarer reddish and black morphs occur, with these colors predominating on the underparts. Hens are larger.

Snail kite (*Rostrhamus sociabilis*): 18in (46cm)
Ranges from the Everglades of Florida south through Central America west of the Andes to Argentina. Also on Cuba. Dark gray with a white area under the tail. The bare skin from the black bill to around the eyes is reddish, becoming more colorful in the breeding season, but yellow in hens, which also have white striping under the throat. Red irises. Feeds mainly on aquatic snails.

Long-winged harrier

Circus buffoni

These harriers have powerful wings and are believed to fly over the Andes on occasion, and regularly travel long distances when migrating. They are occasionally seen well outside what is usually regarded as their normal range, with individuals having been sighted on the Falkland Islands as well as at Tierra del Fuego. Long-winged harriers are most likely to be encountered in relatively open countryside, often in marshland and similarly wet environments.

Identification: Normal color form has a whitish area around the eyes and bill, with a further white necklace of markings beneath. Chest and wings are predominantly blackish, with white underparts. Grayish barring on the flight feathers and tail. There is also a melanistic form, in which the white plumage is replaced by black, apart from on the rump. Female has brownish rather than black plumage and is significantly larger.

Distribution: South America, from southwest Colombia eastward to French Guiana, through parts of Brazil to Argentina, eastern Bolivia and central Chile.
Size: 22in (56cm).
Habitat: Relatively open, lowland tropical areas.
Nest: Concealed on the ground in rushes.
Eggs: 2–4, whitish.
Food: Small vertebrates.

CONDORS AND OTHER BIRDS OF PREY

*The birds featured here include the birds of prey most closely linked with America, in the guise
of the two species of condor, as well as the bald eagle, symbol of the USA. The Californian condor ranks
as one of the rarest birds in the world. There is also the roadrunner, which, thanks to its unusual
habits, has become famous worldwide as a cartoon character.*

Andean condor

Vultur gryphus

Andean condors are the
only vultures from
America to show clear
sexual dimorphism.
With a potential lifespan
measured in decades, and
a correspondingly slow
breeding cycle, pairs are
only likely to rear a
chick in alternate years.
In spite of their strong
bills, which allow them
to rip open carcasses
without difficulty, Andean
condors are not active
hunters. In coastal areas they
scour seal colonies, sometimes
descending in large numbers
to scavenge when food is readily available.

Identification: Massive, vulture-
like appearance. The bare skin
on the cock's head is red, and
black in the larger hen. Cock birds
also display a prominent comb on
the head, as well as a wattle that
is absent in hens. There is a ruff
of white feathering below,
encircling the neck. The rest of
the plumage is predominantly
black aside from the grayish-
white areas on the wings.

Distribution: Andean region
of South America, right down
this mountain range from
Venezuela to Tierra del Fuego
in the far south.
Size: 51in (130^1/$_2$cm).
Habitat: Open mountainous
terrain, but sometimes near
sea level, where these birds
seek carcasses of marine
animals. Prefers to be well
away from human habitation.
Nest: Caves on cliffs.
Eggs: 1, white.
Food: Carrion.

Californian condor

Gymnogyps californianus (E)

These majestic birds used to soar
effortlessly on the thermals,
covering huge distances in search
of large carcasses in true vulture
fashion, but heavy persecution
brought them to the very edge of
extinction. Collisions with
powerlines also reduced their
numbers, until the species was
virtually extinct. The last
remaining wild Californian
condors were caught in 1987 and
integrated into a highly expensive
captive-breeding program, carried
out at zoological collections in
Los Angeles and San Diego. Five
years later, the first birds bred in
captivity were released back into the wild, and
other releases have followed. It takes about eight years
for these condors to attain sexual maturity.

Identification: Huge size,
predominantly black with
white areas on and under
the wings. Bare,
variable pinkish-
orange skin on the
head and neck.
This entire
area of bare
skin is gray
in young
birds.
Sexes
alike.

Distribution: Area north
of Los Angeles, California.
Releases carried out around
the San Joaquin Valley in
California; birds are fitted
with radio telemetry
equipment to track
movement.
Size: 53in (134^1/$_2$cm).
Habitat: Lightly wooded
terrain.
Nest: Usually in caves.
Eggs: 1, white.
Food: Carrion.

Roadrunner

Geococcyx californianus

These unusual members of the cuckoo clan are built for speed. Their common name derives from their habit of frequenting roads that attract lizards and other reptiles to bask on the heat of the tarmac early in the day to raise their body temperature. Roadrunners can run at speeds up to 23mph (37km/h), and although they can fly, they rarely take to the wing. They have a distinct zygodactyl foot structure, with two toes directed forward and two behind, which may assist their balance, compared with the more usual 3:1 perching configuration. Their calls resemble the cooing of doves, and they also communicate by bill-chattering.

Distribution: Southwestern parts of the USA, across from California into Mexico.
Size: 24in (61cm).
Habitat: Open country, including desert areas.
Nest: Low platform of sticks.
Eggs: 4–10, white.
Food: Insects, lizards and small snakes.

Identification: Loose, ragged, dark crest spotted with white. Streaked upper chest becoming white on the underparts. Back and wings brown with buff and whitish edging to the feathers. Powerful, sharp-tipped bill. Gray rump and long tail. Strong legs. Sexes are alike.

Crested caracara (common caracara, *Caracara plancus*): 23in (58^1/$_2$cm)
Occurs in southern USA south through Central America across South America to Tierra del Fuego and the Falkland Islands. Black cap and crest on the head, with whitish area beneath becoming barred on the back and chest. Wings and abdomen show more blackish coloration. Bare, reddish skin on the face. Hens are slightly larger.

Puna hawk (variable hawk, gurney's hawk, *Buteo poecilochrous*): 24in (61cm)
Occurs in the Andean region from southern Colombia south to Chile and Argentina. Exists in both light and dark morphs. Light-colored cocks have whitish underparts and gray upperparts, and the flight feathers are blackish at their tips. The tail is white with dark speckling and a black bar. Hens have a chestnut area at the top of the wings. The entire body aside from the tail is dark slate-gray in the case of the dark morph. Hens are distinguishable from cocks by the chestnut feathering extending over the upper breast, with black-and-white barring on the lower underparts.

Turkey vulture (*Cathartes aura*): 32in (81cm)
Ranges across much of the USA south through Central America and across much of the southern continent. Also occurs on islands ranging from the Greater Antilles in Central America to the Falkland Islands off the coast of southern South America. North American population moves south in the winter. Can find carcasses by scent, and feeds mainly on mammals. Bare, reddish-pink head and brownish-black plumage with slight iridescence. Variation in size through its wide range. Sexes alike.

Bald eagle

Haliaeetus leucocephalus

Distribution: From the Aleutian Islands and Alaska east across Canada and south across the USA into northern Mexico.
Size: 38in (96^1/$_2$cm).
Habitat: Areas where there are large stretches of water.
Nest: Often huge, located in a tree or sometimes on the ground.
Eggs: 1–3, white.
Food: Vertebrates and some carrion, especially in the winter when hunting is more difficult.

The national symbol of the USA, the bald eagle is a highly adaptable species, and is encountered as far north as the freezing tundra of Canada and south to the searing desert heat of Mexico. Feeding habits are diverse; these eagles tend to catch fish during the summer months, switching at other times of the year to birds as large as geese, which are seized in flight. They hunt both by sight and sound, and are drawn to areas where sea otters are feeding by recognizing their calls. The species remains far more common in the northern part of its range, where it has been subject to less habitat disturbance.

Identification: Distinctive white head and tail, yellow bill and talons. Remainder of the plumage is predominantly brown, with lighter edging to some of the feathers on the back and wings. Female is larger, and young birds have dark bills.

Above: Bald eagles may migrate more than 1,250 miles (2,000km).

HUMMINGBIRDS AND JAYS

*One of the unique sights of America is the presence of hummingbirds feeding in backyards,
either from flowers or special feeders. These birds are a source of fascination as they hover in flight
and feed, demonstrating their remarkable aerial agility. However, they may not always be resident
throughout the year, with some species moving to a warmer climate for the winter.*

Ruby-throated hummingbird

Archilochus colubris

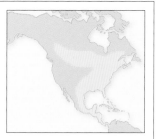

Distribution: Breeds in
eastern North America,
moving southward to Florida
and southwestward to Texas,
through Central America to
Panama for the winter.
Sometimes seen in the
adjoining region of
the Caribbean.
Size: 3½in (9cm).
Habitat: Lightly wooded
areas with flowering plants.
Nest: Cup built in trees
bound with spiders' silk.
Eggs: 2, white.
Food: Nectar, pollen, sap
and invertebrates.

The small
size of these
hummingbirds
is no barrier
to flying long
distances, which
they do back and
forth to their wintering
grounds each year. Cock
birds usually arrive back in
their breeding areas about a week
before the hens are seen in May. Staying in temperate
areas would mean that these birds would have difficulty
finding sufficient plant nectar to sustain them through the
winter. In fact, ruby-throated hummingbirds are far less
specialized in their feeding habits than some members of
this family, and have been recorded feeding on more than
31 different types of plant, although they display a
preference for red flowers. Hens build their nest alone,
binding it with the silk threads of spiders' webs, and are
responsible for rearing the chicks on their own. Tiny
invertebrates feature prominently in their diet at this stage.

Identification: Metallic, greenish-
bronze upperparts. Has a large
glossy red area of plumage under
the throat. The remainder of the
underparts are whitish. Hens are
similar in appearance, but they
have a dusky white area on their
throat instead of the glossy red
patch of the cocks.

Anna's hummingbird

Calypte anna

These hummingbirds are sometimes
seen feeding at the holes in tree bark
drilled by sapsuckers (*Sphyrapicus*
species), which results in the plant's
sap oozing, providing an accessible
source of nutrients. At the outset of
the breeding season, males become
very territorial. Soon afterward,
hens begin to seek out suitable nest
sites, which can include human-made
structures, such as electric wires. They
gather small lengths of plant fibers and
bind them together with silk from spiders'
webs. Lichens are used to fill in gaps
between the stems, and the cup is lined with
feathers. The chicks leave the nest for the first
time when only 18 days old.

Identification: Mostly rose-colored head, with a
bronzy-green area behind the eyes and a small white
spot evident here as well. Upperparts are a shade of
metallic, bronzy green, and underparts are green and
whitish. Hens lack the rose-colored plumage on the
head, and have a brownish throat.

Distribution: Western USA,
from California and offshore
islands southeastward to
Arizona; may move to
southern Oregon during the
winter. Sometimes even
recorded in Alaska.
Size: 4in (10cm).
Habitat: Generally woodland
areas with flowers.
Nest: Cup-shaped.
Eggs: 2, white.
Food: Nectar, pollen, sap
and invertebrates.

Steller's jay

Cyanocitta stelleri

Ranging over a vast area,
Steller's jay has
proved to be a
highly adaptable
species. In some areas,
such as at picnic sites in the Rocky Mountains
in Colorado, these jays have become very tame,
accepting food from people. Elsewhere, they are
much shyer. They eat a varied diet; where food is
likely to be hard to find because of snow in winter,
they forage for acorns in the autumn, which are then
stored for later use. Family groups may remain
together over the winter in northern areas, and the
young leave in the spring when the adult pair start
to nest again. Mud is often used rather like cement to
anchor the bulky nest of twigs together.

Identification: Dark, grayish-blue head
and back, with blue underparts. Tail and
wings are blue with black barring. North
American variety have darker coloration
and more prominent crests than those
occurring further south, which have a
much bluer appearance. Sexes alike.

Distribution: The largest
distribution of all North
American jays, extending
from Alaska south through
Central America to Nicaragua.
Size: 13in (33cm).
Habitat: Woodland and
forest.
Nest: Mound of twigs.
Eggs: 2–6, greenish or bluish
with brown spotting.
Food: Omnivorous.

Black-chinned hummingbird (purple-throated
hummingbird, *Archilochus alexandri*): 4in (10cm)
Breeding range extends from southwest British
Columbia across southern USA into Mexico. Moves
further south over the winter. Black area merging
into broader purple area on the sides of the face and
throat. Underparts are buffy brown, and upperparts
are dull bronzy green. Hen is similar, also with a
white stripe behind the eyes, and buffy on the sides
of the face and throat.

Broad-tailed hummingbird (*Selasphorus
platycercus*): 4½in (11cm)
Breeding range from California through Texas into
southern Mexico and Guatemala. Winters entirely in
Central America. Wide tail feathers. Metallic, deep
reddish-purple throat and sides of the face, with
buffy-brown underparts and metallic green
upperparts. Hens are duller, with brown speckling on
the buffy throat plumage.

Rivoli's hummingbird (magnificent hummingbird,
Eugenes fulgens): 5in (13cm)
Breeding range from southern Arizona and New
Mexico in the USA, with these birds wintering
in Mexico. A separate population in Central America
ranges as far south as western Panama. Deep
purple coloration on the head, becoming blackish
with a white spot behind the eyes, and a brilliant
green throat. Hens have lighter brown underparts.
Light green upperparts in both sexes.

Blue jay (*Cyanocitta cristata*): 12in (30cm)
Eastern North America down to Florida, with
southerly populations being smaller. Blue crest,
white area on the face, edged by black feathering.
Wings are blue with distinctive white markings.
Black barring extends from the flight feathers to the
tail. Underparts are white. Sexes are alike.

Green jay

Inca jay *Cyanocorax yncas*

These woodland birds are found in two
distinct populations. Birds forming the
northern population are better known as
green jays, while the southerly and more
social Andean races are usually described
as Inca jays. One of the most unusual
features of these jays is their habit of
seeking out smoking areas of woodland,
not only in search of small creatures that
may be escaping the flames, but also to
hold their wings out, allowing the smoke
to permeate their plumage. This action is
believed to kill off parasites such as lice
that may be lurking on their bodies.
Young green jays may remain with their
parents and help to rear the new chicks
before establishing
their own territories.

Distribution: Northern
population extends from
Texas to Honduras, while the
separate South American
form ranges from Colombia
to Ecuador.
Size: 10½in (27cm).
Habitat: Woodland and forest.
Nest: Platform of twigs and
similar material.
Eggs: 3–5, grayish lilac with
dark speckling.
Food: Omnivorous.

Identification:
Green plumage is
characteristic. The northern
race has a combination of blue
and black plumage on the head,
being green elsewhere, and
underparts, including the
underside of the tail are
yellowish. Iris is black. South
American race has a pronounced
blue crest above the bill, and pale
green plumage extending right
over the forehead. Iris is yellow.
Sexes are alike.

BACKYARD VISITORS

Although none of these birds is brightly colored, most have a lively song that draws attention to their presence. Some develop into regular bird-table visitors and can become quite tame as a result. They are generally lively and active by nature, irrespective of their size. A number of their species undertake seasonal movements, especially those found in the far north.

Tufted titmouse

Parus bicolor

Distribution: Eastern North America, from southern Ontario south to the Gulf of Mexico, although not present in southern Florida. Range appears to be expanding in some areas of Canada.
Size: 6in (15cm).
Habitat: Light, deciduous woodland.
Nest: Small tree holes and nest boxes.
Eggs: 3–8, creamy white with brown spots.
Food: Invertebrates in summer; seeds during winter.

This is the largest member of the tit family occurring in America. It is quite conspicuous through its range, thanks in part to its noisy nature. The vocal range of male tufted titmice is especially varied, and individuals are able to sing more than 15 different song patterns. Hens also sing, but not to the same extent and mainly during spring and early summer. The range of these titmice has increased northward, largely because bird-table offerings guarantee them food throughout the year. In the south, they have been recorded as hybridizing with black-crested titmice (*P. atricristatus*) in central parts of Texas. The resulting offspring have grayish crests and a pale orange band above the bill. In spite of their small size, these titmice are determined visitors to bird tables, driving off much larger species. They can be equally fierce in defending their nests.

Identification: Characteristic black band immediately above the bill, with gray crest and crown. Cheeks and underparts are whitish, with pale reddish-orange flanks. Sexes alike. Young birds are duller overall, with less contrast in their plumage.

Above: The nest cup of this tit is lined with soft material.

Carolina chickadee

Parus carolinensis

This species is very closely related to the black-capped chickadee (*P. atricapillus*), which occurs further north, and it is not unknown for the birds to hybridize where they overlap. Studies of their song patterns have revealed that the Carolina chickadee has a four-note call, whereas the black-capped has a two-note whistle. Although pairs have their own territories during the summer, Carolina chickadees form larger groups in the winter months. During cold weather, they spend much longer periods of time roosting in tree hollows to conserve their body heat, sometimes remaining there for up to 15 hours per day. This is also the time of year when chickadees are most likely to be seen visiting bird tables in search of food.

Identification: Black area extends to the back of the head, with black under the bill, broadening across the throat. White on the sides of the face. Underparts are whitish with a slightly orange cast. Wings and tail are primarily grayish olive. Sexes alike.

Distribution: Northeastern USA south to Texas and northern Florida. Occasionally recorded in Ontario, Canada.
Size: 5in (12½cm).
Habitat: Light, broad-leaved woodland.
Nest: In small holes in trees, also uses nest boxes.
Eggs: 3–9, white with reddish-brown spots.
Food: Invertebrates and seeds.

Bushtit (*Psaltriparus minimus*): 4¹/₂in (11cm)
Ranges from British Columbia in Canada south and eastward through the USA to parts of Mexico and Guatemala in Central America. Three groupings are recognized. The northern common bushtit has brownish ear coverts, brown cap and gray upperparts, with paler, more whitish underparts. Hens have grayer throats. In the lead-colored variety, gray coloration extends onto the cap. In the Central American black-eared form, cock birds have black areas on the sides of the face.

House wren (*Troglodytes aedon*): 5in (13cm)
Southern Canada through Central America as far as Argentina. Birds in northern parts of the range move south for the winter. Grayish upperparts, brown wings and tail with black barring. Lighter underparts. Pale ring around the eye and no striping on the head. Sexes are alike.

Northern mockingbird (*Mimus polyglottos*): 11in (28cm)
Southern Canada through the USA to southern Mexico and the Caribbean. Relatively dull, with gray upperparts, paler on the underparts. Broad white area on the wings, most apparent in flight. Sexes are alike.

Red-breasted nuthatch (*Sitta canadensis*): 4¹/₂in (11cm)
Southeast Alaska and Canada into western and northeastern USA. May move south in the winter. Black areas on the head, separated by a white line, with gray on the wings. Underparts are rusty orange. Hens similar but distinguished by their gray head coloration.

Cactus wren

Campylorhynchus brunneicapillus

This is a surprisingly large wren that is often seen in the vicinity of cacti, building its bulky nest of dried grass within the protective spines of these plants or thornbushes. The calls of the cactus wren have a decidedly monotonous tone, consisting simply of the sound "chut" repeated over and over again. The cactus wren does not raise its tail vertically in true wren fashion, but holds it horizontally. These birds prefer to remain near the ground, flying low and hunting for invertebrates there. Nests near the ground are concealed so they are less apparent to predators.

Identification: Brown area on the top of the head extending over the nape, with a white stripe passing through the eye, and white streaking on the back. Prominent black spotting on the breast, becoming more streaked on the pale underparts. Barring apparent on the wings and tail. Sexes are alike.

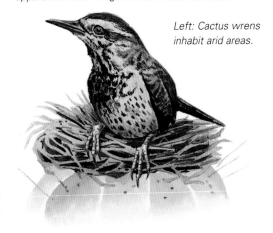

Left: Cactus wrens inhabit arid areas.

Distribution: Southwestern USA from California southward as far as central Mexico.
Size: 8¹/₂in (22cm).
Habitat: Arid areas and desert.
Nest: Large structure made of vegetation.
Eggs: 4–7, creamy white with spots.
Food: Invertebrates.

Catbird

Dumetella carolinensis

The song of these relatives of the mockingbird incorporates a sound like a cat's miaowing, and is the reason for their common name. Catbirds also possess a harsher alarm call in their vocal repertoire. They can often be heard singing after dark, especially on moonlit nights. Catbirds are quite shy by nature, and their coloration also helps them to blend into the background. Their chestnut underparts are most conspicuous during the cock's display, when he chases the hen in the early stages of courtship. When on the move, the catbird flicks its long tail repeatedly. Insects are a vital part of catbirds' diet, especially when they are rearing chicks, since the insects provide valuable protein. Catbirds may catch their insect prey above water, and these birds are often observed in areas close to ponds and streams.

Identification: Slate-gray in color, with a distinctive black cap. Also has chestnut underparts, which may not be clearly visible. Sexes alike.

Distribution: Southern Canada south and eastward across the USA to central Florida, moving south in the winter as far as Panama and Cuba.
Size: 9in (23cm).
Habitat: Scrubland, hedgerows and gardens.
Nest: Loosely constructed cup of vegetation.
Eggs: 4–6, glossy blue green.
Food: Fruit and insects.

SONGBIRDS

Many of these birds are a common sight, thanks to their adaptable natures. They often undertake seasonal movements southward to a warmer climate in search of more favorable feeding opportunities over the winter period. Their return is keenly anticipated, however, as an indicator of the arrival of spring. Pairs will then breed perhaps twice before returning south again.

Virginian cardinal

Northern cardinal *Cardinalis cardinalis*

The range of these cardinals continues to increase both in northern and western areas, especially since the first breeding record from Canada, which dates back to 1901. This expansion probably results from bird-table offerings. The stout, conical bill of these birds is adapted to crushing seeds, although Virginian cardinals will also hunt invertebrates, particularly when they have chicks in the nest.

Distribution: From southern Ontario, Canada, south through the USA to the Gulf of Mexico, and southward as far as Belize.
Size: 9in (23cm).
Habitat: Edges of woodland, parks and backyards.
Nest: Cup-shaped, made of vegetation.
Eggs: 3-4, whitish or grayish white, with darker spots and blotches.
Food: Seeds and invertebrates.

Identification: Predominantly red, with a pointed crest. A black mask surrounds the bill extending back to the eyes and down onto the throat. Wings, back and tail are of a slightly duller shade. Hen is predominantly brown, with a slight reddish suffusion over the wings and tail. The bill in adults of both sexes is bright red, whereas that of young birds is blackish, enabling them to be distinguished from adult hens.

Scarlet tanager

Piranga olivacea

These tanagers undertake long flights each year to and from their breeding grounds. Individuals sometimes venture further afield, and are observed in more northerly and westerly areas than usual, even reaching Alaska on rare occasions. A pair of scarlet tanagers rears only one brood during the summer before returning south. These birds catch invertebrates in the undergrowth and also in flight. More unusually, scarlet tanagers rub live ants onto their plumage. This behavior, known as anting, results in formic acid being released by the ants among the feathers, which in turn drives out parasites, such as lice, from the plumage. The birds' bright coloration is linked in part to their diet.

Identification: Mainly yellowish olive, with underparts being more yellowish than upperparts. Cock distinguishable from the hen by having black rather than brownish wings and tail. In breeding plumage, the male has characteristic vivid scarlet plumage. Young cock birds in their first year have more orange rather than scarlet plumage.

Distribution: Migrates north to southeastern Canada and eastern USA, overwintering in Central and South America, east of the Andes to Peru and Bolivia.
Size: 7in (18cm).
Habitat: Light forest and woodland.
Nest: Cup-shaped, made of stems and roots.
Eggs: 2–5, whitish to greenish blue with dark markings.
Food: Mainly invertebrates.

Blue grosbeak

Guiraca caerulea

In spite of the cock bird's distinctive plumage, the blue grosbeak is not as conspicuous as its coloration would suggest. Indeed, in poor light its feathering can appear so dark that, at a distance, it is sometimes confused with the male common cowbird (*Molothius ater*). The grosbeak's melodious song is most commonly heard early in the day, although the birds may start singing again at dusk. The song consists largely of short notes interspersed with longer trills. Cock birds usually return from their winter haunts a few days ahead of hens, frequently spending this time searching for food in groups on the ground before splitting up to nest. Pairs are likely to rear two broods of chicks over the summer period before migrating south again during September.

Identification: A dull shade of blue, with a large, grayish bill. The wings are darker, with two distinctive wing bars close to the shoulder. Hens are predominantly brownish, lighter on the underparts, and also display two buff-colored wing bars. They have some bluish feathering on the rump. Young cock birds have more widespread blue feathering among their plumage.

Distribution: Occurs widely across the USA, from California in the west through to New Jersey on the east coast, and south to Costa Rica. Northern populations overwinter in Central America, ranging from Mexico to Panama.
Size: 7½in (19cm).
Habitat: Brush, often near water.
Nest: Cup-shaped.
Eggs: 3–4, pale blue.
Food: Seeds and invertebrates.

American robin (*Turdus migratorius*): 11in (28cm)
Ranges from Alaska and Canada in summer south across much of the USA and through Central America to southern Mexico. Chestnut-reddish plumage on the breast and upper abdomen, with white below. Upperparts are predominantly grayish. White area around the eye and striping under the throat. Hens are significantly paler and browner in appearance.

Eastern bluebird (*Sialia sialis*): 7in (18cm)
Ranges from southern Canada to the Gulf states and Arizona, extending as far south as Nicaragua. Migrates south from northern areas for the winter, staying no further north at this stage than southern parts of New England and southern Michigan. Blue head, wings and tail are offset against rusty-red breast feathering, which becomes whiter on the abdomen. Hens are duller, with more grayish-blue upperparts. Young birds are brown and speckled, with areas of whitish and some blue plumage.

Cedar waxwing (*Bombycilla cedrorum*): 7in (18cm)
Southeast Alaska and Canada to southern-central parts of the USA. Ranges further south into Panama over the winter. Brown, pointed crest with black stripe from the sides of the bill through the eyes to the back of the head. Small white area back from the base of the lower bill. Remainder of the plumage is mainly olive green with yellower underparts. Tail is gray with yellow tips. Distinctive red, wax-like coloring on the secondary flight feathers (which is why these birds are known as waxwings) but no white is evident here. Sexes are alike.

American goldfinch

Carduelis tristis

These attractive songbirds are common throughout their range, although those in northern areas move south to warmer areas for the winter. They are often seen in larger flocks at this time, frequently in the company of related birds such as redpolls (*Acanthis* species). Their diet varies through the year, and is influenced by the availability of food. Invertebrates, which provide protein, are important for rearing chicks in the nest. Seeds are consumed through much of the year, while shoots and buds of trees such as spruce and willow will be eaten when other foods are in short supply.

Distribution: Canada southward through much of the USA to northern Mexico.
Size: 5½in (14cm).
Habitat: Wooded or lightly wooded areas.
Nest: Cup-shaped.
Eggs: 2–7, pale blue.
Food: Seeds, other plant matter and invertebrates.

Identification: Brightly colored yellow plumage, with a black cap and black wings and tail, and white bars on the wings. Duller in winter plumage, being a more olive shade, with a far less distinct black cap. Hens can be recognized by their olive-yellow upperparts and more yellowish underparts, becoming brownish during winter, especially on the upperparts. The white wing barring is still apparent, enabling hens to be distinguished easily from juveniles.

GLOSSARY

avifauna: The birds of a specified region or period of time.

breeding plumage: The often brightly colored plumage that the cock birds of some species adopt before breeding.

carpal: The area of plumage at the top of the leading edge of the wings.

cere: The fleshy area, encompassing the nostrils, located above the bill. Often especially prominent in parrots.

columbiforms: The group of birds that comprises doves and pigeons.

contour feathers: The smaller feathers covering the head and body.

corvid: A member of the Corvidae family, such as crows, ravens and jays.

coverts: The specific contour feathers covering the wings and base of the tail.

cryptic: Refers to coloration or formation that conceals or camouflages.

culmen: The central ridge of the bill.

down: Plumage of a loose texture that primarily serves to conserve body heat.

eclipse plumage: A transitional plumage seen, for example, in the drakes of some ducks, occurring after they have molted their breeding plumage.

frugivore: A species that eats mainly fruit.

irruption: An unpredictable movement of large numbers of birds outside their normal range.

lek: An area where the male birds of certain species perform courtship displays.

lores: The area between the bill and the eyes on each side of the face.

mantle: Plumage of the same color occurring on the back and folded wings of certain birds.

melanistic: A dominance of black in the plumage, often in a specific color phase.

migrant: A bird that undertakes regular seasonal movements, breeding in one locality and overwintering in another.

nidicolous: Refers to the chicks of species that remain in the nest for some time after hatching.

nidifugous: Describes the chicks of species that leave the nest immediately after hatching.

nuchal: Plumage at the nape of the neck.

orbital: The skin around the eye.

pectoral: Of or located on the breast.

precocial: Refers to newly hatched young covered with down and fully active.

race: A geographically isolated population below the level of species, which differs slightly, typically in size or color, from other races of the same species.

raptor: A bird of prey that actively hunts its food.

ratite: A large, flightless bird, such as the greater rhea (*Rhea americana*), which has a flat breastbone without the keel-like ridge of flying birds.

scapular: Of or on the shoulder.

spatule: Spoon-shaped or spatula-shaped feathers, on the wing or the tail.

speculum: A distinctive patch of color evident in the flight feathers of certain birds, particularly ducks and parrots.

syrinx: The voice organ of birds, located at the base of the trachea (windpipe).

tarsal: Refers to the area at or below the ankle in birds, as in tarsal spur.

torpidity: A state of dormancy, usually undertaken to conserve energy and combat possible starvation in the face of adverse environmental conditions.

wattle: A wrinkled, fleshy piece of skin hanging from the throat or chin of some birds, or present on the head.

INDEX